new interchange

English for international communication

Jack C. Richards

with Jonathan Hull and Susan Proctor

student's book

2A

New Interchange Student's Book revision prepared by Jack C. Richards.

PUBLISHED BY THE PRESS SYNDICATE OF THE UNIVERSITY OF CAMBRIDGE
The Pitt Building, Trumpington Street, Cambridge, United Kingdom

CAMBRIDGE UNIVERSITY PRESS
The Edinburgh Building, Cambridge CB2 2RU, UK
40 West 20th Street, New York, NY 10011–4211, USA
477 Williamstown Road, Port Melbourne, VIC 3207, Australia
Ruiz de Alarcón 13, 28014 Madrid, Spain
Dock House, The Waterfront, Cape Town 8001, South Africa

http://www.cambridge.org

First published 1997
16th printing 2004

New Interchange Student's Book 2 has been developed from *Interchange* Student's Book 2,
first published by Cambridge University Press in 1991.

Printed in Hong Kong, China

Typeface New Century Schoolbook *System* QuarkXPress® [AH]

A catalog record for this book is available from the British Library

Library of Congress Cataloging in Publication data
Richards, Jack C.
New interchange: English for international communication :
student's book 2 / Jack C. Richards with Jonathan Hull and Susan Proctor.
p. cm.
Rev. ed. of: Interchange : English for international communication :
student's book 2. 1991.
ISBN 0-521-62862-8
1. English language – Textbooks for foreign speakers.
2. Communication, International – Problems, exercises, etc.
I. Hull, Jonathan. II. Proctor, Susan. III. Richards,
Jack C. Interchange. IV. Title.
PE1128.R4593 1997
428.2'4 – dc21 97-27440
CIP

ISBN 0 521 62862 8 Student's Book 2
ISBN 0 521 62861 X Student's Book 2A
ISBN 0 521 62860 1 Student's Book 2B
ISBN 0 521 62859 8 Workbook 2
ISBN 0 521 62858 X Workbook 2A
ISBN 0 521 62857 1 Workbook 2B
ISBN 0 521 62856 3 Teacher's Edition 2
ISBN 0 521 62855 5 Teacher's Manual 2
ISBN 0 521 62854 7 Class Audio Cassettes 2
ISBN 0 521 62852 0 Student's Audio Cassette 2A
ISBN 0 521 62652 8 Student's Audio Cassette 2B
ISBN 0 521 62853 9 Class Audio CDs 2
ISBN 0 521 62851 2 Student's Audio CD 2A
ISBN 0 521 62850 4 Student's Audio CD 2B
ISBN 0 521 95019 8 Audio Sampler 1–3

Also available
ISBN 0 521 62849 0 Video 2 (NTSC)
ISBN 0 521 62848 2 Video 2 (PAL)
ISBN 0 521 62847 4 Video 2 (SECAM)
ISBN 0 521 62846 6 Video Activity Book 2
ISBN 0 521 62845 8 Video Teacher's Guide 2
ISBN 0 521 63887 9 Video Sampler 1–2
ISBN 0 521 77379 2 Lab Guide 2
ISBN 0 521 77378 4 Lab Cassettes 2
ISBN 0 521 80575 9 Teacher-Training Video with Video Manual
ISBN 0 521 62882 2 New Interchange/Passages Placement and Evaluation Package

Book design, art direction, and layout services: Adventure House, NYC
Illustrators: Adventure House, Randy Jones, Mark Kaufman, Kevin Spaulding, Sam Viviano
Photo researcher: Sylvia P. Bloch

Introduction

THE NEW EDITION

New Interchange is a revision of *Interchange*, one of the world's most successful and popular English courses. *New Interchange* incorporates many improvements suggested by teachers and students from around the world. Some major changes include many new Conversations, Snapshots, and Readings; more extensive Grammar Focus models and activities; a greater variety and amount of listening materials; extensive changes to the **Teacher's Edition** and **Workbook**; and additions to the **Video.**

New Interchange is a multi-level course in English as a second or foreign language for young adults and adults. The course covers the four skills of listening, speaking, reading, and writing, as well as improving pronunciation and building vocabulary. Particular emphasis is placed on listening and speaking. The primary goal of the course is to teach communicative competence, that is, the ability to communicate in English according to the situation, purpose, and roles of the participants. The language used in *New Interchange* is American English; however, the course reflects the fact that English is the major language of international communication and is not limited to any one country, region, or culture. This level is for intermediate students and takes them from the low-intermediate up to the intermediate level.

This level builds on the foundations for accurate and fluent communication already established in prior levels by extending grammatical, lexical, and functional skills. Because the syllabus covered in this Student's Book reviews language features taught at the prior level, students who have not previously used *New Interchange* can successfully study at this level.

COURSE LENGTH

Each full level of *New Interchange* contains between 70 and 120 hours of class instruction time. For classes where more time is available, the Teacher's Edition gives detailed suggestions for Optional Activities to extend each unit. Where less time is available, the amount of time spent on Interchange Activities, Reading, Writing, Optional Activities, and the Workbook can be reduced.

Each split edition contains approximately 35 to 60 hours of classroom material. The Student's Book, Workbook, and Student's Audio Cassettes or CDs are available in split editions.

COURSE COMPONENTS

The **Student's Book** contains 16 six-page units, each divided into two topical/functional "cycles," as well as four review units. At the back of the book are 16 communication tasks, called "Interchange Activities," and summaries of grammar and vocabulary taught in each unit.

The full-color **Teacher's Edition** features detailed teaching instructions directly across from the Student's Book pages, along with audio scripts, cultural notes, answer keys, and optional activities. At the back of the Teacher's Edition are instructions for Interchange Activities, an Optional Activities Index, a Workbook Answer Key, and four photocopiable Achievement Tests with audio scripts and answer keys.

The **Workbook** provides a variety of reading, writing, and spelling exercises to reinforce the grammar and vocabulary taught in the Student's Book. Each six-page unit follows the same teaching sequence as the Student's Book; some exercises recycle teaching points from previous units in the context of the new topic. The Workbook can be used for classwork or homework.

The **Class Audio Program**, available on cassette or CD, is intended for classroom use. The Conversations, Grammar Focus models, Pronunciation exercises, and Listening activities in the Student's Book are all recorded naturally with a variety of native and some nonnative accents. Recorded exercises are indicated with the symbol .

The **Student's Audio Program** provides opportunities for self-study. It contains recordings of all Student's Book exercises marked with the symbol , except for the Listening tasks, which are intended only for classroom use. These tasks appear exclusively on the Class Audio Program and are indicated by the symbol CLASS AUDIO ONLY.

The **Video** offers entertaining dramatic or documentary sequences that review and extend language learned in each unit of the Student's Book. The **Video Activity Book** contains comprehension, conversation, and language practice activities, and the **Video Teacher's Guide** provides instructional support, answer keys, and photocopiable transcripts of the video sequences.

The **CD-ROM**, appropriate for home or laboratory use, offers a wealth of additional practice. Each of the 16 units is based on a sequence from the Video. Four tests help students monitor their progress.

The **Placement Test** helps determine the most appropriate level of *New Interchange* for incoming students. A booklet contains the four-skills test on photocopiable pages, as well as instructions for test administration and scoring. A cassette accompanies the listening section of the test.

The **Lab Cassettes** provide self-study activities in the areas of grammar, vocabulary, pronunciation, listening, and functional use of English. The **Lab Guide** contains photocopiable pages that guide students through the activities.

The **Teacher-Training Video** offers clear guidance for teaching each section of the Student's Book and professional development activities appropriate for individual or group use.

APPROACH AND METHODOLOGY

New Interchange teaches students to use English for everyday situations and purposes related to school, social life, work, and leisure. The underlying philosophy is that learning a second or foreign language is more rewarding, meaningful, and effective when the language is used for authentic communication. Throughout *New Interchange,* students are presented with natural and useful language. In addition, students have the opportunity to personalize the language they learn, make use of their own knowledge and experiences, and express their ideas and opinions.

KEY FEATURES

Adult and International Content *New Interchange* deals with contemporary topics that are of high interest and relevant to both students and teachers. The topics have been selected for their interest to both homogeneous and heterogeneous classes.

Integrated Syllabus *New Interchange* has an integrated, multi-skills syllabus that links topics, communicative functions, and grammar. Grammar – seen as an essential component of second and foreign language proficiency and competence – is always presented communicatively, with controlled accuracy-based activities leading to fluency-based communicative practice. In this way, there is a link between grammatical form and communicative function. The syllabus is carefully graded, with a gradual progression of teaching items.

Enjoyable and Useful Learning Activities A variety of interesting and enjoyable activities provides thorough individual student practice and enables learners to apply the language they learn. The course also makes extensive use of information-gap tasks; role plays; and pair, group, and whole class activities. Task-based and information-sharing activities provide a maximum amount of student-generated communication.

WHAT EACH UNIT CONTAINS

Snapshot The Snapshots graphically present interesting real-world information that introduces the topic of a unit or cycle, and also develop vocabulary. Follow-up questions encourage discussion of the Snapshot material and personalize the topic.

Conversation The Conversations introduce the new grammar of each cycle in a communicative context and present functional and conversational expressions.

Grammar Focus The new grammar of each unit is presented in color boxes and is followed by controlled and freer communicative practice activities. These freer activities often have students use the grammar in a personal context.

Fluency Exercise These pair, group, whole class, or role-play activities provide more personal practice of the new teaching points and increase the opportunity for individual student practice.

Pronunciation These exercises focus on important features of spoken English, including stress, rhythm, intonation, reductions, and blending.

Listening The Listening activities develop a wide variety of listening skills, including listening for gist, listening for details, and inferring meaning from context. Charts or graphics often accompany these task-based exercises to lend support to students.

Word Power The Word Power activities develop students' vocabulary through a variety of interesting tasks, such as word maps and collocation exercises. Word Power activities are usually followed by oral or written practice that helps students understand how to use the vocabulary in context.

Writing The Writing exercises include practical writing tasks that extend and reinforce the teaching points in the unit and help develop student's compositional skills. The Teacher's Edition demonstrates how to use the models and exercises to focus on the process of writing.

Reading The reading passages use various types of texts adapted from authentic sources. The Readings develop a variety of reading skills, including reading for details, skimming, scanning, and making inferences. Also included are pre-reading and post-reading questions that use the topic of the reading as a springboard to discussion.

Interchange Activities The Interchange Activities are pair work, group work, or whole class activities involving information sharing and role playing to encourage real communication. These exercises are a central part of the course and allow students to extend and personalize what they have practiced and learned in each unit.

Unit Summaries Unit Summaries are located at the back of the Student's Book. They contain lists of the key vocabulary and functional expressions, as well as grammar extensions for each unit.

FROM THE AUTHORS

We hope that you will like using *New Interchange* and find it useful, interesting, and fun. Our goal has been to provide teachers and students with activities that make the English class a time to look forward to and, at the same time, provide students with the skills they need to use English outside the classroom. Please let us know how you enjoy it and good luck!

Jack C. Richards
Jonathan Hull
Susan Proctor

Authors' Acknowledgments

A great number of people contributed to the development of *New Interchange*. Particular thanks are owed to the following:

The **reviewers** using the first edition of *Interchange* in the following schools and institutes – the insights and suggestions of these teachers and their students have helped define the content and format of the new edition: Jorge Haber Resque, **Centro Cultural Brasil-Estados Unidos (CCBEU),** Belém, Brazil; Lynne Roecklein, **Gifu University,** Japan; Mary Oliveira and Montserrat M. Djmal, **Instituto Brasil-Estados Unidos (IBEU),** Rio de Janeiro, Brazil; Liliana Baltra, **Instituto Chileno Norte-Americano,** Santiago de Chile; Blanca Arazi and the teachers at **Instituto Cultural Argentino Norteamericano (ICANA),** Buenos Aires, Argentina; Mike Millin and Kelley Seymour, **James English School,** Japan; Matilde Legorreta and Manuel Hidalgo, **Kratos, S.A. de C.V.,** Mexico D.F.; Peg Donner, Ricia Doren, and Andrew Sachar, **Rancho Santiago College Centennial Education Center,** Santa Ana, California, USA; James Hale, **Sundai ELS,** Japan; Christopher Lynch, **Sunshine College,** Tokyo, Japan; Valerie Benson, **Suzugamine Women's College,** Hiroshima, Japan; Michael Barnes, **Tokyu Be Seminar,** Japan; Claude Arnaud and Paul Chris McVay, **Toyo Women's College,** Tokyo, Japan; Maria Emilia Rey Silva, **UCBEU,** São Paulo, Brazil; Lilia Ortega Sepulveda, **Unidad Lomoa Hermosa,** Mexico D.F.; Eric Bray, **Kyoto YMCA English School,** Kyoto, Japan; John Pak, **Yokohama YMCA English School,** Yokohama, Japan; and the many teachers around the world who responded to the *Interchange* questionnaire.

The **editorial** and **production** team: Suzette André, Sylvia P. Bloch, John Borrelli, Mary Carson, Karen Davy, Samuela Eckstut, Randee Falk, Andrew Gitzy, Christa Hansen, Pauline Ireland, Stephanie Karras, Penny Laporte, Kathy Niemczyk, Kathleen Schultz, Rosie Stamp, and Mary Vaughn.

And Cambridge University Press **staff** and **advisors**: Carlos Barbisan, Kathleen Corley, Kate Cory-Wright, Riitta da Costa, Peter Davison, Peter Donovan, Robert Gallo, Cecilia Gómez, Colin Hayes, Thares Keeree, Jinsook Kim, Koen Van Landeghem, Alex Martinez, Carine Mitchell, Chuanpit Phalavadhana, Sabina Sahni, Helen Sandiford, Dan Schulte, Ian Sutherland, Chris White, Janaka Williams, and Ellen Zlotnick.

Plan of Book 2A

Title/Topics	Functions	Grammar
UNIT 1 PAGES 2–7		
A time to remember People; childhood; reminiscences	Introducing yourself; talking about yourself; exchanging personal information; remembering your childhood; asking about someone's childhood	Past tense; *used to* for habitual actions
UNIT 2 PAGES 8–13		
Caught in the rush Transportation; transportation problems; city services	Talking about transportation and transportation problems; evaluating city services; asking for and giving information	Adverbs of quantity with countable and uncountable nouns: *too many, too much, not enough, more, fewer, less*; indirect questions from *Wh*-questions
UNIT 3 PAGES 14–19		
Time for a change! Houses and apartments; lifestyle changes; wishes	Describing positive and negative features; making comparisons; talking about lifestyle changes; expressing wishes	Evaluations and comparisons with adjectives: *not . . . enough, too, not as . . . as, as . . . as*; Evaluations and comparisons with nouns: *not enough . . ., as many . . . as*; *Wish*
UNIT 4 PAGES 20–25		
I've never heard of that! Food; recipes; instructions; cooking methods	Talking about food; expressing likes and dislikes; describing a favorite snack; giving instructions	Simple past vs. present perfect; sequence adverbs: *first, then, next, after that, finally*
REVIEW OF UNITS 1–4 PAGES 26–27		
UNIT 5 PAGES 28–33		
Going places Travel; vacations; plans	Describing vacation plans; giving travel advice; planning a vacation	Future with *be going to* and *will*; modals for necessity and suggestion: *(don't) have to, must, need to, better, ought to, should*
UNIT 6 PAGES 34–39		
Sure. No problem! Complaints; household chores; requests; excuses; apologies	Making requests; accepting and refusing requests; complaining; apologizing; giving excuses	Two-part verbs; *will* for responding to requests; requests with modals and *Would you mind . . .?*
UNIT 7 PAGES 40–45		
What's this for? Technology; instructions	Describing technology; giving instructions; giving advice	Infinitives and gerunds; infinitive complements
UNIT 8 PAGES 46–51		
Let's celebrate! Holidays; festivals; customs; celebrations	Describing holidays, festivals, customs, and special events	Relative clauses of time; adverbial clauses of time: *before, when, after*
REVIEW OF UNITS 5–8 PAGES 52–53		

1 A time to remember

1 SNAPSHOT

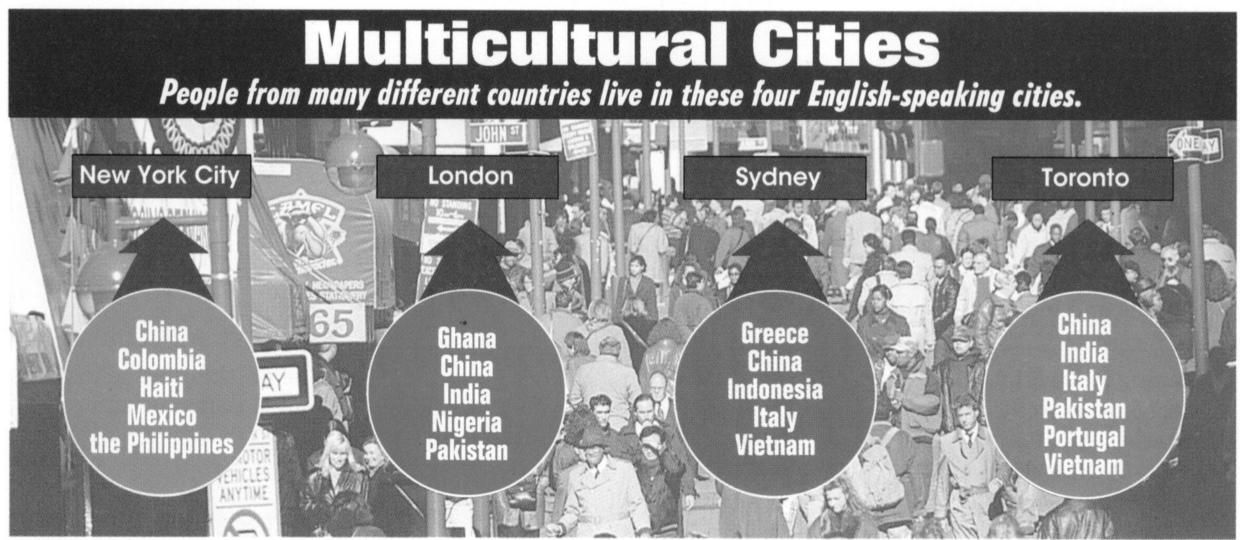

Multicultural Cities
People from many different countries live in these four English-speaking cities.
New York City
China
Colombia
Haiti
Mexico
the Philippines
London
Ghana
China
India
Nigeria
Pakistan
Sydney
Greece
China
Indonesia
Italy
Vietnam
Toronto
China
India
Italy
Pakistan
Portugal
Vietnam

Source: UN Department for International, Economic, and Social Affairs

Talk about these questions.

Why do you think these cities have so many immigrants?
Are there any immigrants in your city? Where are they from originally?

2 CONVERSATION

A Listen and practice.

Ted: Oh, I'm really sorry. Are you OK?
Ana: I'm fine. But I'm not very good at this.
Ted: Neither am I. Say, are you from South America?
Ana: Yes, I am, originally. I was born in Argentina.
Ted: Did you grow up there?
Ana: Yes, I did, but my family moved here eight years ago, when I was in high school.
Ted: And where did you learn to Rollerblade?
Ana: Here in the park. This is only my second time.
Ted: Well, it's my *first* time. Can you give me some lessons?
Ana: Sure. Just follow me.
Ted: By the way, my name is Ted.
Ana: And I'm Ana. Nice to meet you.

B Listen to the rest of the conversation. What are two more things you learn about Ted?

3 GRAMMAR FOCUS

Past tense

Where **were** you born?	I **was** born in South America.
Were you born in Brazil?	No, I **wasn't.** I **was** born in Argentina.
Where **did** you **grow** up?	I **grew** up in Buenos Aires.
When **did** you **move** here?	I **moved** here eight years ago, when I was in high school.
Did you **learn** Spanish in high school?	No, I **didn't.** I **studied** it in college.
Did you **go** to college in California?	Yes, I **did.** I **went** to college in Los Angeles.

A Complete these conversations. Then practice with a partner.

1. A: Could you tell me a little about yourself? Where .... you born?
   B: I .... born in South Korea.
   A: .... you grow up there?
   B: No, I .... I .... up in Canada.

2. A: Where .... you .... to high school?
   B: I .... to high school in Ecuador.

3. A: .... you study English when you .... a child?
   B: Yes, I ....
   A: How old .... you when you began to study English?
   B: I .... eleven years old.

B ***Pair work*** Take turns asking the questions in part A. Give your own information when answering.

4 LISTENING

Listen to interviews with two immigrants to the United States. Complete the chart.

	Yu Hong	Ajay
1. Where is he/she from?	....	....
2. When did he/she move to the United States?	....	....
3. What does he/she do now?	....	....
4. What is difficult about being an immigrant?	....	....
5. What does he/she miss the most?	....	....

5 GETTING TO KNOW YOU

A ***Pair work*** Interview a classmate you don't know very well. Ask questions like the ones below and take notes. Start like this:

A: Hi! My name's . . . .
B: Hello. I'm . . . . Nice to meet you.
A: Good to meet you, too. Could you tell me a little about yourself?
B: Sure. What do you want to know?
A: Well, where were you born?

Where were you born?
Did you grow up there?
Where did you go to elementary school?
Where did you go to high school?
Did you study any foreign languages?
When did you first study English?
When did you graduate?
How old were you when you moved to . . . ?

B ***Class activity*** Use your notes and introduce your partner to the class. Start like this:

"I'd like to introduce Angela. She was born in Mexico, but she grew up in a small town near Monterey, California."

6 WORD POWER *When I was a child . . . .*

A Complete the word map. Add one more word to each category. Then compare with a partner.

beach
bicycle
cat
collect comics
dog
paint
play chess
rabbit
scrapbook
soccer ball
summer camp
tree house

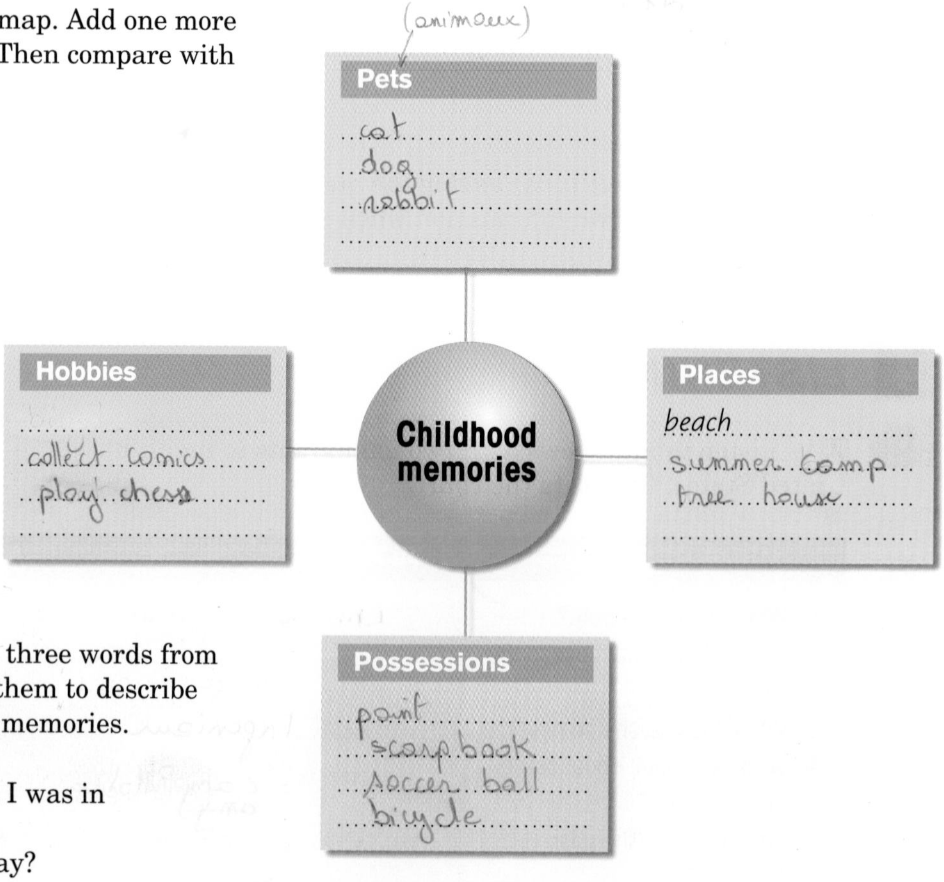

Childhood memories

Pets
....
....
....
....

Hobbies
....
....
....
....

Places
beach
....
....
....

Possessions
....
....
....
....

B ***Pair work*** Choose three words from the word map and use them to describe some of your childhood memories.

A: I played chess when I was in elementary school.
B: How well did you play?
A: I was pretty good.

7 CONVERSATION

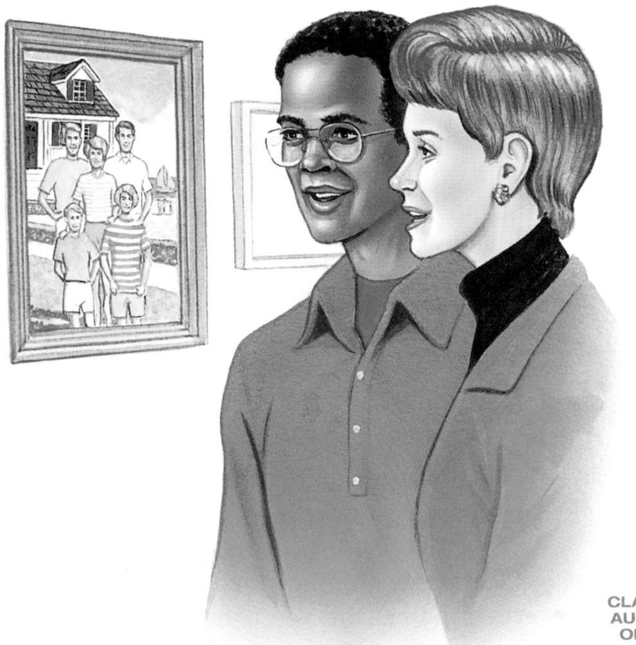

A Listen and practice.

Jeff: Hey! Are these pictures of you when you were a kid?
Kim: Yeah. That's me in front of my uncle's beach house. When I was a kid, we used to spend two weeks there every summer.
Jeff: Wow, I bet that was fun!
Kim: Yeah. We always had a great time. Every day we used to get up early and walk along the beach. I had a great shell collection. In fact, I think it's still up in the attic!
Jeff: Hey, I used to collect shells, too, when I was a kid. But my parents threw them out!

CLASS AUDIO ONLY **B** Listen to the rest of the conversation. What is Jeff's favorite childhood memory?

8 GRAMMAR FOCUS

Used to

Used to refers to something that you regularly did in the past but don't do anymore.

When I was a kid, we **used to** stay at my uncle's beach house.

Did you **use to** have a hobby?
Yes, I **used to** collect shells.

What games **did** you **use to** play?
I **used to** play chess.

A Complete these sentences. Then compare with a partner.

1. In elementary school, I used to . . . .
2. I used to be . . . , but I'm not anymore.
3. When I was a kid, I used to play . . . .
4. After school, my best friend and I used to . . . .

B ***Pair work*** Write five more sentences about yourself using *used to*. Do you and your partner have anything in common?

9 PRONUNCIATION Used to

A Listen and practice. Notice the pronunciation of **used to**.

When I was a child, I **used to** play the violin.
I **used to** have a nickname.
I **used to** have a pet.
I **used to** play hide-and-seek.

B *Pair work* Practice the sentences you wrote in Exercise 8 again. Pay attention to the pronunciation of **used to**.

10 MEMORIES

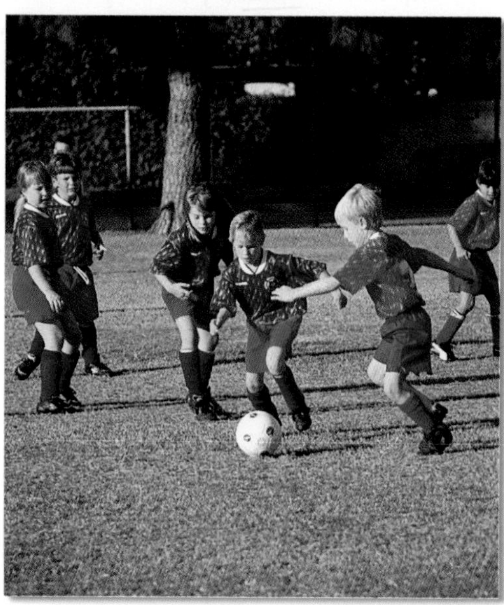

A *Pair work* Add three questions to this list. Then take turns asking and answering the questions.

1. What's your favorite childhood memory?
2. What sports or games did you use to play when you were younger?
3. Did you use to have a nickname?
4. Where did you use to spend your vacations?
5. Did you ever have a part-time job?
6. ....
7. ....
8. ....

B *Class activity* Tell the class two interesting things about your partner.

11 WRITING

A Write about the things you used to do as a child. Use some of your ideas from Exercise 10.

When I was four years old, my family moved to Oregon.
We had an old two-story house and a big yard to play in.
My older brother and I used to play lots of games together.
In the summer, my favorite outdoor game was hide-and-seek.
It was both fun and scary because we . . . .

B *Group work* Take turns reading your compositions aloud. Answer any questions from the group.

interchange 1
Class profile
Find out about your classmates. Turn to page IC-2.

12 READING

Joan Chen

Do you know these film terms?
actor/actress agent director film studio producer (leading) part

a scene from *The Last Emperor*

Joan Chen is famous both in China, where she grew up, and in the United States, where she now lives. How did Joan become a famous actress in two countries? It's an interesting story.

Joan Chen was born in Shanghai in 1961. When she was 14, some people from a film studio came to her school and chose her to study at the studio. She was happy about this chance, but mainly she liked the idea of getting out of school. Soon, however, she discovered that she really liked acting. At age 18, she won the Golden Rooster, China's top film award.

In the late 1970s, Joan's parents, who were doctors, moved to the United States. Joan joined them when she was 20 and went to college there. Her parents hoped she would study medicine. Instead, she majored in film and later looked for work as an actress. To work in the United States, Joan had to start all over again. She told Hollywood agents that she was an actress in China, but she only got some small parts in TV shows.

One day Joan went to speak to a director who was making a movie called *Tai-Pan*. The interview didn't go well. As she walked away, a man in a car noticed her. The man was Dino DeLaurentiis, the film's producer. He immediately offered her a leading part. A year later, she starred in Bernardo Bertolucci's *The Last Emperor* and was on her way to worldwide fame.

A Read the article. Then put the events in Joan Chen's life into the correct order (1–8).

.... won the Golden Rooster
.... appeared in *Tai-Pan*
.... left school and studied at a film studio
.... starred in *The Last Emperor*
.... studied film in college
.... moved to the United States
....1.... was born in China in 1961
.... got her first part in a TV show

B ***Group work*** Talk about these questions.

1. Do parents and children often have different ideas about careers? How are their ideas different?
2. Why is it sometimes difficult for people who move to another country to keep doing the same work?

2 Caught in the rush

1 WORD POWER *Compound nouns*

A Match the nouns in columns A and B to make compound nouns. (More than one answer is possible.)

subway + entrance = subway entrance

A	*B*
subway	entrance
traffic	stop
bus	light
bicycle	station
stop	sign
parking	lane
street	stand
news	jam
taxi	space

a subway entrance

a traffic light

B *Pair work* How many compound nouns can you make beginning with these words?

police   telephone   fire   train

2 CONVERSATION

A Listen and practice.

Lynn: Why is there never a bus when you want one?
Sam: Good question. There aren't enough buses on this route.
Lynn: Sometimes I feel like writing a letter to the paper.
Sam: Good idea. You should say that we need more subway lines, too.
Lynn: Yeah. There should be more public transportation in general.
Sam: And fewer cars! There's too much traffic.
Lynn: Say, is that our bus coming?
Sam: Yes, it is. But look. It's full!
Lynn: Oh, no! Let's go and get a cup of coffee. We can talk about this letter I'm going to write.

B Listen to the rest of the conversation. What else is wrong with the transportation system in their city?

3 GRAMMAR FOCUS

Adverbs of quantity

With countable nouns	*With uncountable nouns*
There are **too many** cars.	There is **too much** traffic.
There are**n't enough** buses.	There is**n't enough** parking.
We need **more** subway lines.	We need **more** public transportation.
There should be **fewer** cars.	There should be **less** pollution.

A Complete these statements about transportation problems. Then compare with a partner. (More than one answer may be possible.)

1. There are ...too many... police officers.
2. There should be ...fewer...... cars in the city.
3. There isn't enough... public transportation.
4. The government needs to build ...more........ highways.
5. There should be ...less.......... noise.
6. We should have ...more....... public parking garages.
7. There is ...more........ air pollution in the city.
8. There are ......many..... cars parked on the streets.

B *Group work* Complete these statements about the city you are living in. Then compare with others.

1. The city needs to provide more . . . .
2. We have too many . . . .
3. There's too much . . . .
4. There should be fewer . . . .
5. We don't have enough . . . .
6. There should be less . . . .

4 LISTENING

A Listen to someone talk about how Singapore has tried to solve its traffic problems. Check (✓) True or False for each statement.

	True	False
1. Motorists are never allowed to drive into the business district.	☐	✓
2. People need a special certificate to be able to buy a car.	✓	☐
3. Cars cost much more than they do in the United States and Canada.	✓	☐
4. Public transportation still needs to be improved.	☐	✓

B Listen again. For the statements that you marked false, write the correct information.

C *Class activity* Could the solutions adopted in Singapore work in your city? Why or why not?

5 YOU BE THE JUDGE!

A ***Group work*** How would you rate the transportation services in your city? Complete the chart. Give each item a rating from 1 to 5.

1 = terrific 2 = good 3 = average (OK) 4 = needs improvement 5 = terrible

.... the train system	.... taxi service	.... the bus system
.... facilities for pedestrians	.... the subway system	.... parking

B ***Class activity*** Explain your ratings to the class.

"We gave taxi service a rating of 4. We think the city needs more taxis and cheaper fares. Also, taxi drivers should be more polite."

Making the city better

Suggest ways to improve a city. Turn to page IC-3.

6 WRITING

Write a paragraph about transportation in your city.

Public transportation is good in my city. We have an excellent bus system. The traffic moves quickly, except at rush hour. However, we need more public parking. There aren't enough parking spaces downtown, so it always takes too much time to find a space.

7 SNAPSHOT

Source: *World Book Encyclopedia*

Talk about these questions.

Have you used any of these kinds of transportation?
Are there any unusual forms of transportation in your city or country?
What kinds of transportation do you usually use?

8 CONVERSATION

A Listen and practice.

Erica: Excuse me. Could you tell me where the bank is?
Man: There's one upstairs, across from the duty-free shop.
Erica: Oh, thanks. Do you know what time it opens?
Man: It should be open now. It opens at 8:00 A.M.
Erica: Good. And can you tell me how often the buses leave for the city?
Man: You need to check at the transportation counter. It's right down the hall.
Erica: OK. And just one more thing. Do you know where the nearest restroom is?
Man: Right behind you, ma'am. See that sign?
Erica: Oh. Thanks a lot.

B Listen to the rest of the conversation.
Check (✓) the information that Erica asks for.

- ☐ the cost of a taxi to the city
- ☐ the location of the taxi stand
- ☐ the location of a cash machine
- ☐ the location of a restaurant

9 GRAMMAR FOCUS

Indirect questions from Wh-questions

Wh-questions with **be**	*Indirect questions*
Where is the bank?	Could you tell me **where the bank is?**
Where is the taxi stand?	Do you know **where the taxi stand is?**
Wh-questions with **do** *or* **did**	*Indirect questions*
How often do the buses leave for the city?	Can you tell me **how often the buses leave for the city?**
When did Flight 566 arrive?	Do you know **when Flight 566 arrived?**
What time does the duty-free shop open?	Do you know **what time the duty-free shop opens?**

A Write indirect questions using these Wh-questions.
Then compare with a partner.

1. How much does a newspaper cost?
2. Where is the nearest cash machine?
3. What time do the banks open?
4. How often do the buses come?
5. Where can you get a good hamburger?
6. How late do the nightclubs stay open?

B ***Pair work*** Take turns asking the questions you wrote in part A.
Give your own information when answering.

A: Do you know how often the buses come?
B: Every half hour.

10 PRONUNCIATION Question intonation

A Listen and practice. Wh-questions usually have falling intonation. Indirect questions usually have rising intonation.

What time does the duty-free shop open?

Can you tell me what time the duty-free shop opens?

Where is the taxi stand?

Do you know where the taxi stand is?

B Practice these questions. Pay attention to question intonation.

Where is Adam Street?
Could you tell me where Adam Street is?
What time does the department store open?
Do you know what time the department store opens?

11 TOURISTS

A ***Pair work*** What would a tourist visiting your city ask about? Think of six questions about transportation, accommodations, sightseeing, and other services in your city.

B ***Group work*** Take turns asking and answering your questions.

A: Can you tell me where the Golden Pavilion is?
B: Let me think. Oh, yes, it's . . . .

useful expressions

Let me think. Oh, yes, ...
I'm not really sure, but I think . . . .
Sorry, I don't know.
It's close to/near . . . .
It's on the corner of . . . .
It's next to . . . .

Golden Pavilion, Kyoto, Japan

12 READING

Stuck in an Airport?
What to do . . .

What do people usually do while they're waiting in an airport?

Many people are upset when their flight is delayed. Not only do they have to change their schedule but, even worse, they have to wait in an airport! There's no need to be upset, though. Airports are much better places these days than most people realize.

- **Belief:** Airport food is bad – as bad as airplane food.
- **Reality:** Airports have fine international cuisine – from fresh seafood in London to Korean barbecue in Honolulu. And you can stock up on something to have for later – for example, cheese and caviar in Paris.

Heathrow Airport, London

Schiphol Airport, Amsterdam

- **Belief:** Shopping in airports is great, that is, if you need a T-shirt.
- **Reality:** In Amsterdam, you can buy anything from perfume to diamonds. In El Paso, Texas, you can buy antique knives or regional art. The art is so interesting that some people fly to El Paso just to visit the airport gallery. And Singapore's airport is known for some of the best shopping in the world!

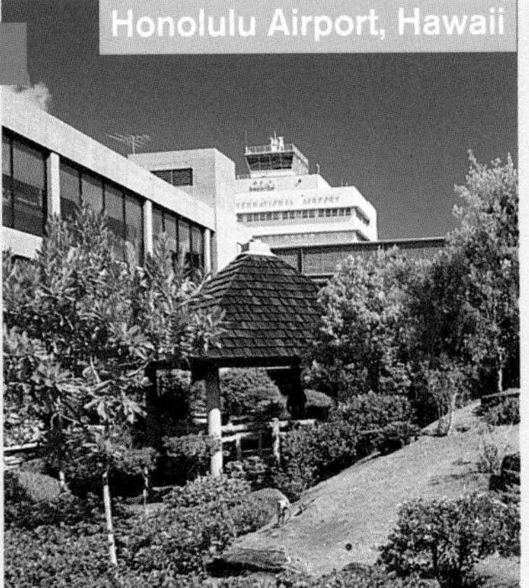
Honolulu Airport, Hawaii

- **Belief:** Airports make people uncomfortable and tense.
- **Reality:** The airport at Honolulu has peaceful gardens. Pittsburgh has a meditation room: When you walk in, relaxing music comes on and pictures of clouds are projected on the walls. If you prefer exercise, hotels at the airports in Los Angeles, Dallas, and many other cities have fitness centers that anyone can use.

So, the next time you're stuck in an airport, have some fun!

A Read the article. In which airport can you do the following? Write the letter of the correct place.

1. meditate surrounded by music and clouds ....
2. eat Korean barbecue ....
3. buy an interesting painting ....
4. exercise in a fitness center ....
5. buy a diamond ....
6. visit one of the world's best shopping places ....

a. Amsterdam
b. Dallas
c. Singapore
d. Honolulu
e. Pittsburgh
f. El Paso

B ***Group work*** Talk about these questions.

1. Which airport mentioned in the article would you prefer to wait in? Why?
2. Imagine your flight is delayed. What would you prefer to do: eat, shop, or relax? Anything else?

3 Time for a change!

1 WORD POWER *Houses and apartments*

A These adjectives are used to describe houses and apartments. Which words are positive? Which are negative?
Write **P** or **N** next to each word.

bright	......	dingy	......	private	......
comfortable	......	expensive	......	quiet	......
convenient	......	huge	......	safe	......
cramped	......	inconvenient	......	shabby	......
dangerous	......	modern	......	small	......
dark	......	noisy	......	spacious	......

B ***Pair work*** Tell your partner two positive and two negative features about your house or apartment.

"My apartment is very dark and a little cramped. However, it's in a safe neighborhood and it's very private."

2 CONVERSATION *Apartment hunting*

A Listen and practice.

Mr. Dean: What do you think?
Mrs. Dean: Well, it has just as many bedrooms as the last apartment. And the living room is huge.
Jenny: But the bedrooms are too small. And there isn't enough closet space for my clothes.
Mr. Dean: And it's not as cheap as the last apartment we saw.
Mrs. Dean: But that apartment was dark and dingy. And it was in a dangerous neighborhood.
Mr. Dean: Let's see if the real estate agent has something else to show us.

B Listen to the Deans talk about another apartment.What does Jenny like about it? What doesn't she like?

3 GRAMMAR FOCUS

Evaluations and comparisons

Evaluations with adjectives	*Evaluations with nouns*
The kitchen is**n't** big **enough**. The living room is **too** small.	There are**n't enough** bedrooms. There is**n't enough** closet space.
Comparisons with adjectives	*Comparisons with nouns*
It's **not as** cheap **as** the last apartment. It's **almost as** cheap (**as** the last apartment).	It doesn't have **as many** bedrooms **as** the last apartment. It has **just as many** bedrooms (**as** the last apartment).

A Read the opinions about these apartments. Then rephrase the opinions using the words in parentheses.

Spacious, modern apartment
2 bedrooms, 1 bathroom; very private; located outside the city; 2-car garage; $800 per month.

Older, small apartment
2 bedrooms, 2 bathrooms; located downtown, by the commuter train; 1 parking space; $800 per month.

Apartment 1

1. There are only a few windows. (not enough)
2. It's not bright enough. (too)
3. It has only one bathroom. (not enough)
4. It's not convenient enough. (too)

"There aren't enough windows."

Apartment 2

5. It's not spacious enough. (too)
6. It's too old. (not enough)
7. It isn't quiet enough. (too)
8. There's only one parking space. (not enough)

B Write comparisons of the apartments using the words below and *as . . . as*. Then compare with a partner.

Apartment 1	*Apartment 2*
bright	big
bedrooms	expensive
bathrooms	modern

Apartment 1 isn't as bright as Apartment 2.

C ***Pair work*** Compare living in an apartment to living in a house. Which would you prefer to live in?

A: A house is not as expensive as an apartment.
B: Yes, but an apartment is too small for a large family.

4 PRONUNCIATION Sentence stress

A Listen and practice. Stress the words in a sentence that carry the most important information.

The a**part**ment isn't **big** enough.
The **kit**chen is **too** cramped.

There **aren't** enough **clo**sets. placard
There **isn't** enough **light.**

B *Pair work* Practice the sentences you wrote in part A of Exercise 3. Pay attention to sentence stress.

5 LISTENING

A Listen to three people call about apartment advertisements. Check (✓) the words that best describe each apartment.

1.		2.		3.	
☐ quiet	☑ noisy	☐ spacious	☑ small	☐ expensive	☑ reasonable
☑ spacious	☐ cramped	☑ convenient	☐ inconvenient	☐ safe	☐ dangerous
☐ modern	☑ old	☑ quiet	☐ noisy	☑ dark	☐ light

B Listen again. Do you think each caller is going to rent the apartment? Why or why not?

6 SNAPSHOT

Common Wishes People Have About Their Lives
add more hours to every day
change my appearance
improve my personality
move to a new place
enjoy life more
go back to school
become healthier
get a different job
make new friends

Based on interviews with adults between 18 and 50

Talk about these questions. I wish I felt better

Which of these things would you like to do? Give some examples.
What other things would you like to change about your life? Why?

- I wish I could move now
- I wish I had enough money
- I wish I could buy this cars

7 CONVERSATION *Making wishes*

A Listen and practice.

Brian: So where are you working now, Terry?
Terry: Oh, I'm still at the bank. I don't like it, though.
Brian: That's too bad. Why not?
Terry: Well, it's boring, and it doesn't pay very well.
Brian: I know what you mean. I don't like my job either. I wish I could find a better job.
Terry: Actually, I don't want to work at all anymore. I wish I had a lot of money so I could retire now.
Brian: Hmm, how old are you, Terry?
Terry: Uh, twenty-six.

B Listen to the rest of the conversation. What other changes would Brian and Terry like to make?

8 GRAMMAR FOCUS

Wish

Wish *is followed by past tense forms but refers to the present.*

Fact	*Wish*
I don't like my job.	I **wish** (that) I **could find** a better job. I **wish** I **worked** somewhere else.
I live with my parents.	I **wish** I **lived** in my own apartment. I **wish** I **didn't live** with my parents.
Life is difficult.	I **wish** it **were*** easier. I **wish** it **weren't** so difficult.

**After* wish, were *is used with* I, he, she, *and* it.

Write a response using *wish* for each statement. Then compare with a partner. (More than one answer is possible.)

1. My class is boring.
2. I have to take the bus to work every day.
3. Our apartment is too small.
4. I have too much homework.
5. I'm not in good shape.
6. I'm single.
7. I don't have enough money.
8. I don't have any free time.

I wish my class were more interesting.
I wish that I could take another class.

9 LISTENING

A Listen to four people talk about things they wish they could change. Check (✓) the topic each person is talking about.

Topic			
1. ☐ apartment ☑ job	2. ☑ leisure ☐ school	3. ☑ skills ☐ hobbies	4. ☐ interests ☑ appearance

Wishful thinking

Find out about your classmates' wishes. Turn to page IC-4.

B Listen again. What change would each person like to make? Why?

10 TIME FOR A CHANGE

A What do you wish were different about these situations? Write down your wishes. Then compare with a partner.

your appearance	your school or job	your skills
your family	your home	your free time

B ***Group work*** Choose two of your wishes from part A. Take turns talking about your wishes and how you would make the necessary changes.

A: I wish I could change my job.
B: Really?
A: Yes. I'd like to be a musician.
C: A musician? Wow!
A: I'd like to play the guitar in a rock band.
I could take guitar lessons. And then . . . .

11 WRITING

A Write about one of your wishes from Exercise 10.

I wish I had more free time. I take classes all day, and I have a part-time job in the evening. At home, I spend my time studying or doing chores around the house. I'd like to have more time to read and go out with my friends.

B ***Pair work*** Take turns reading your compositions with a partner. Give your partner suggestions for making the change.

12 READING

Dreams Can Come True

Do you know anyone who made a big change in his or her lifestyle?

At the age of 40, Tom Bloch was the head of H&R Block, a huge company that helps people prepare their tax forms. He was very successful. Although Bloch earned a lot of money, he wasn't very happy: He spent too much time at work and didn't have enough time to spend with his family. Suddenly, he left H&R Block and became a teacher in a poor neighborhood. "I wanted to . . . help people who didn't have the opportunities I had," Bloch explained.

Learning to control the students was hard at first. But the rewards – helping children and hearing students say he's their favorite teacher – are great. And Bloch is able to spend more time with his family.

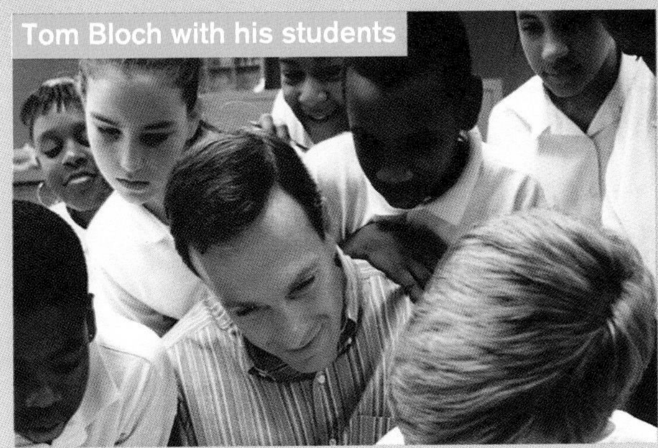
Tom Bloch with his students

the Neale family

For eleven years, Tom Neale worked as a lawyer, and his wife, Mel, worked as a teacher; they saved every penny they could. Finally, they had enough money to buy a boat. That was seventeen years ago, and, except for occasional stops, they have been at sea ever since.

For the Neales and their two daughters, the difficulties of their lifestyle are very real: There's not much money, so meals are often rice and beans (and fish!). Storms are dangerous, especially when the boat is far from land. But Tom Neale says overcoming dangers together as a family is one of the rewards of their way of life. Another, he says, is "seeing the starfish on the bottom of the sea in the moonlight."

A Read the article. What do these people do now? What is one difficulty with their new lifestyles? What is one reward? Complete the chart.

	What they do now	Difficulty	Reward
1. Tom Bloch	....	....	....
2. the Neales	....	....	....

B *Group work* Talk about these questions.

1. Who do you think made the more difficult change in lifestyle, Tom Bloch or the Neales? Explain your answer.
2. Would you like to be one of the Neales' children? Why or why not?
3. What are some reasons people – those in the article and others – change their lifestyles?
4. Would you like to change your lifestyle? If so, how?

4 I've never heard of that!

1 SNAPSHOT

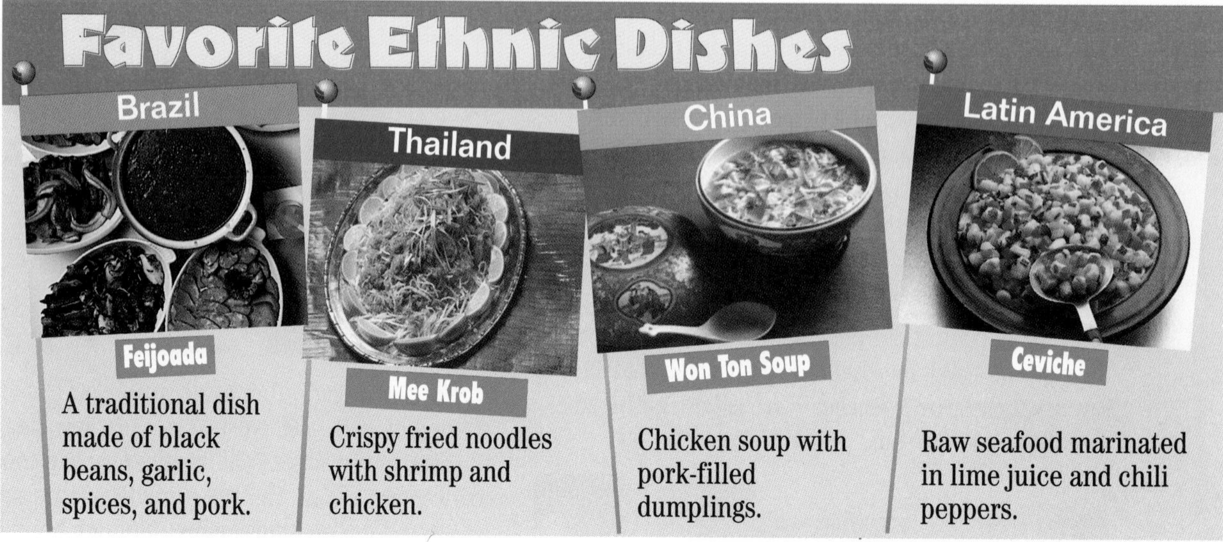

Favorite Ethnic Dishes
Brazil
Feijoada
A traditional dish made of black beans, garlic, spices, and pork.
Thailand
Mee Krob
Crispy fried noodles with shrimp and chicken.
China
Won Ton Soup
Chicken soup with pork-filled dumplings.
Latin America
Ceviche
Raw seafood marinated in lime juice and chili peppers.

Sources: *Fodor's South America, Fodor's Southeast Asia, World Book Encyclopedia*

Talk about these questions.

Have you ever tried any of these dishes? Which ones would you like to try?
What other ethnic food can you try in your city?
What are three popular dishes in your country?

2 CONVERSATION

A Listen and practice.

Kathy: Hey, this sounds good – snails with garlic! Have you ever eaten snails?
John: No, I haven't.
Kathy: Oh, they're delicious! I had them last time. Like to try some?
John: No, thanks. They sound strange.
Waitress: Have you decided on an appetizer yet?
Kathy: Yes. I'll have the snails, please.
Waitress: And you, sir?
John: I think I'll have the fried brains.
Kathy: Fried brains? Now that really sounds strange!

B Listen to the rest of the conversation. How did John like the fried brains? What else did he order?

3 PRONUNCIATION Reduced forms

Listen and practice. Notice how **did you** and **have you** are pronounced in these questions.

Did you skip breakfast this morning?
Did you cook your own dinner last night?

Have you ever tried Indian food?
Have you ever eaten snails?

4 GRAMMAR FOCUS

Simple past vs. present perfect

Simple past: completed events at a definite time in the past	*Present perfect: events within a time period up to the present*
Did you **eat** snails at the restaurant last night? No, I **didn't**.	**Have** you ever **eaten** snails? No, I **haven't**.
Did you **go** out for dinner on Saturday? Yes, I **did**.	**Have** you **been** to a French restaurant? **Yes**, I **have**.
I **went** to a Korean restaurant last week.	I**'ve never been** to a Greek restaurant.

A Complete these conversations. Then practice with a partner. (See the appendix for help with verb forms.)

1. A: Have you ever .... (be) to a picnic at the beach?
   B: Yes, I .... It was fun!
2. A: Did you .... (have) dinner at home last night?
   B: No, I .... I .... (go) out for dinner.
3. A: Have you .... (try) sushi?
   B: No, I .... , but I'd like to.
4. A: Did you .... (have) breakfast this morning?
   B: Yes, I .... I .... (eat) a huge breakfast.
5. A: Have you ever .... (eat) at a Mexican restaurant?
   B: Yes, I .... The food was delicious!

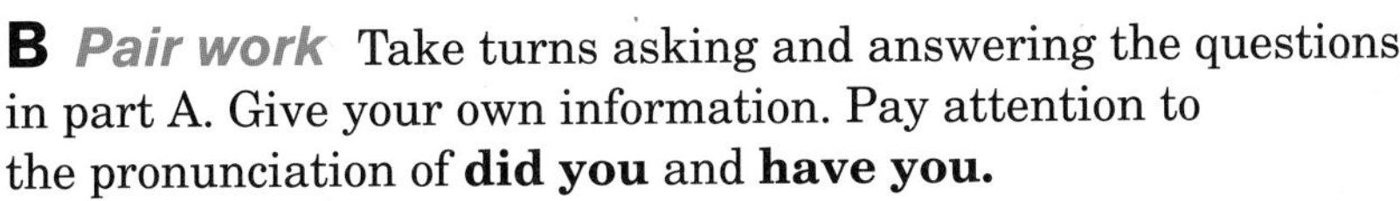

B *Pair work* Take turns asking and answering the questions in part A. Give your own information. Pay attention to the pronunciation of **did you** and **have you.**

5 LISTENING

CLASS AUDIO ONLY

Listen to six people ask questions about food and drink in a restaurant. Check (✓) the item that each person is talking about.

1.	2.	3.	4.	5.	6.
☑ water	☐ coffee	☐ soup	☐ coffee	☐ cake	☑ the check
☐ bread	☑ the meal	☑ pasta	☑ the meat	☑ coffee	☐ the menu

6 BUSYBODIES

Pair work Ask your partner these questions and four more of your own. Then ask follow-up questions.

Did you . . . ?

make your own breakfast this morning
go out for dinner last week
eat a big lunch yesterday

Have you ever . . . ?

tried frog's legs
been on a diet
cooked a large dinner for some friends

A: Did you make your own breakfast this morning?
B: Yes, I did.
A: What did you make?
B: I made scrambled eggs.

Risky business
Find out some interesting facts about your classmates.
Turn to page IC-5.

7 WORD POWER *Cooking methods*

A How do you cook these foods? Check (✓) the methods that are most common in your country. Then compare with a partner.

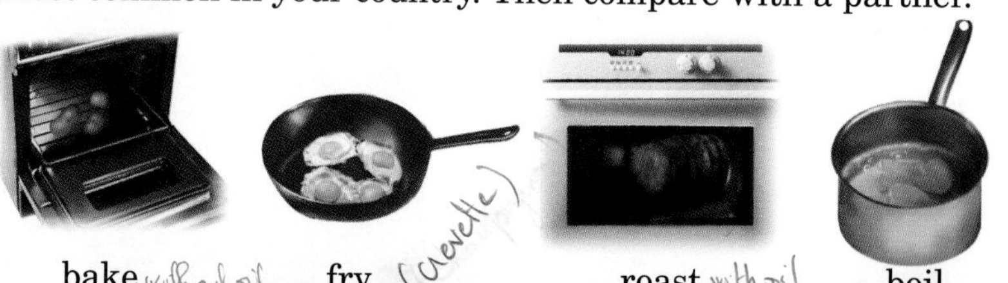

bake fry roast boil barbecue steam

Methods	Foods								
	fish	shrimp	eggs	chicken	beef	potatoes	onions	eggplant	bananas
bake	☒	☒	☐	☒	☒	☒	☒	☒	☒
fry	☒	☐	☒	☒	☒	☒	☐	☒	☒
roast	☒	☒	☐	☒	☒	☒	☒	☒	☒
boil	☑	☒	☒	☒	☒	☒	☒	☒	☐
barbecue	☒	☐	☐	☑	☒	☒	☒	☒	☒
steam	☒	☒	☒	☑	☒	☒	☒	☒	☐

B What's your favorite way to cook the foods in part A?

A: I usually like to steam fish.
B: I prefer to bake it.

8 CONVERSATION

A Listen and practice.

Kate: What's your favorite snack?
Jim: Oh, it's a sandwich with peanut butter, honey, and a banana. It's really delicious!
Kate: Ugh! I've never heard of that! How do you make it?
Jim: Well, first, you take two slices of bread and spread peanut butter on them. Then cut a banana into small pieces and put them on one of the slices of bread. Finally, pour some honey over the bananas and put the other slice of bread on top. Yum!
Kate: Yuck! It sounds awful!

B Listen to the rest of the conversation.
What is Kate's favorite snack? Would you like to try it? Why or why not?

9 GRAMMAR FOCUS

Sequence adverbs

First, spread peanut butter on two slices of bread.
Then cut a banana into small pieces.
Next, put the pieces of banana on one slice of bread.
After that, pour honey over the bananas.
Finally, put the other slice of bread on top.

A Here's a recipe for barbecued kebobs. Look at the pictures and number the sentences from 1 to 5. Then add a sequence adverb to each step.

☐ .... put the meat and vegetables on the skewers.
☐ .... put charcoal in the barbecue and light it with lighter fluid.
☐ .... take the kebobs off the barbecue and enjoy!
☐ .... put the kebobs on the barbecue and cook for 10 to 15 minutes, turning them over from time to time.
☐ .... cut up some meat and vegetables and put them in a bowl with your favorite barbecue marinade. Marinate for 20 minutes.

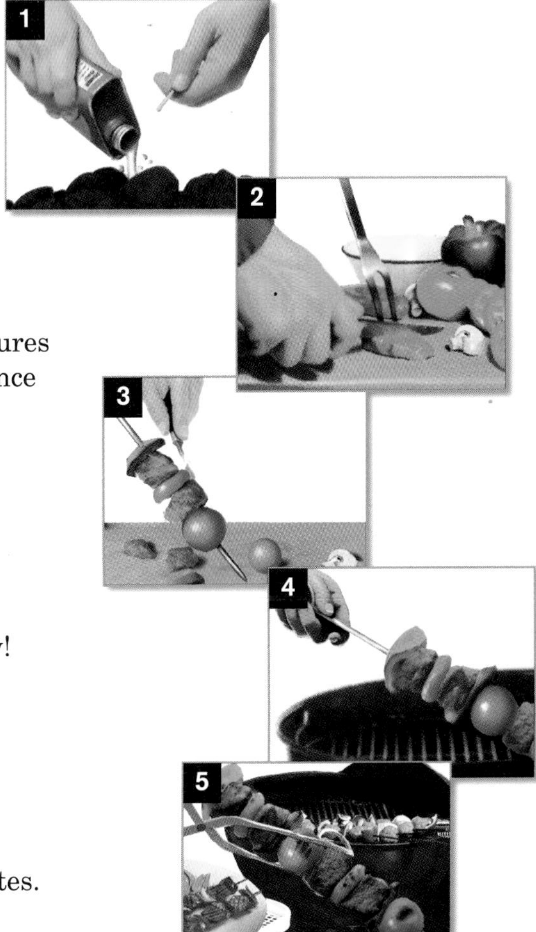

B *Pair work* Cover the recipe and look only at the pictures. Explain each step of the recipe to your partner.

Fat ≠ thin

10 TEMPTING SNACKS

A Listen to people explain how to make these snacks. Which snack are they talking about? Number the photos (1–4).

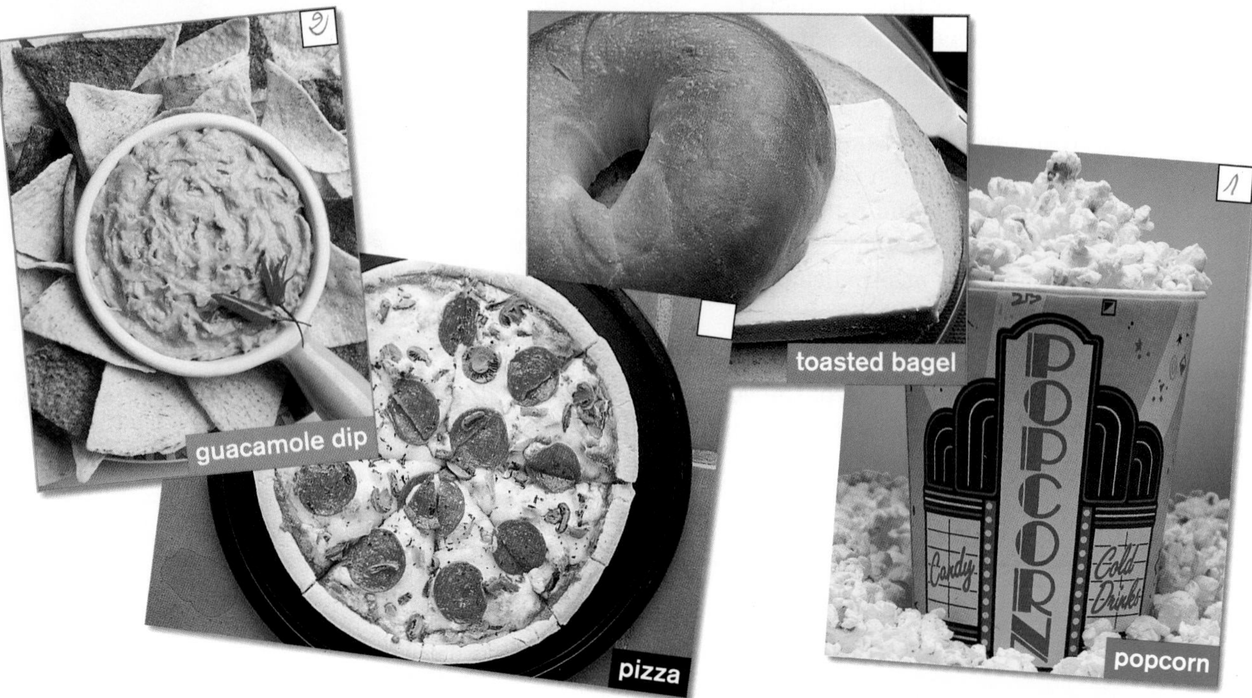

guacamole dip

pizza

toasted bagel

popcorn

B *Pair work* Choose one of the recipes you heard about in part A. Can you remember how to make it? Compare with your partner.

C *Group work* Take turns describing how to make your favorite snack. Then tell the class about the most interesting one.

A: What's your favorite snack?
B: It's . . . .
C: What ingredients do you need to make it?
B: You need . . . .
A: How do you make it?
B: Well, first, you . . . . After that, ... Next, ... Then . . . .

11 WRITING Recipes

A Write a recipe for an interesting dish. First, list the ingredients you need. Then describe how to make the dish.

This recipe is for chicken curry. For this dish, you need chicken, coconut milk, ...
First, cut up the chicken. Then fry the chicken pieces in oil . . . .

B *Group work* Exchange recipes and read them. Is there a recipe you would like to try? Why?

12 READING

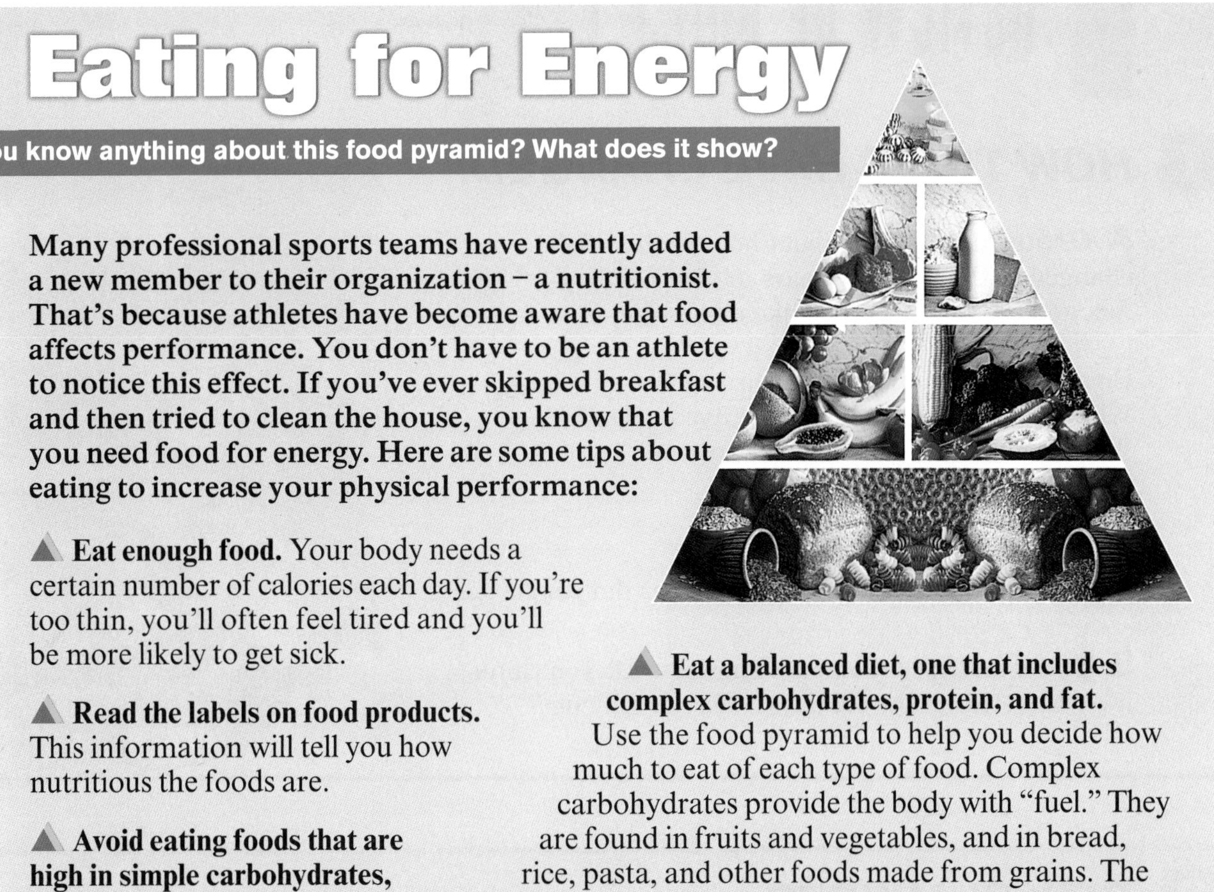

Eating for Energy

Do you know anything about this food pyramid? What does it show?

Many professional sports teams have recently added a new member to their organization – a nutritionist. That's because athletes have become aware that food affects performance. You don't have to be an athlete to notice this effect. If you've ever skipped breakfast and then tried to clean the house, you know that you need food for energy. Here are some tips about eating to increase your physical performance:

▲ **Eat enough food.** Your body needs a certain number of calories each day. If you're too thin, you'll often feel tired and you'll be more likely to get sick.

▲ **Read the labels on food products.** This information will tell you how nutritious the foods are.

▲ **Avoid eating foods that are high in simple carbohydrates, that is, sugars.** A chocolate bar will first give you energy, but then it will leave you feeling even more tired.

▲ **Eat a balanced diet, one that includes complex carbohydrates, protein, and fat.** Use the food pyramid to help you decide how much to eat of each type of food. Complex carbohydrates provide the body with "fuel." They are found in fruits and vegetables, and in bread, rice, pasta, and other foods made from grains. The body uses protein to build muscles, and it uses fat to absorb the vitamins in food. Protein and fat are found in foods like milk, cheese, meat, fish, and eggs. Too much fat, however, can be harmful.

A Read the article and look at the food pyramid. Then check (✓) True or False. For the statements that you marked false, write the correct information.

	True	False
1. You shouldn't eat foods that are high in complex carbohydrates.	☐	☑
2. Fruits and vegetables are a good source of protein.	☑	☐
3. A person should eat more carbohydrates than fat or protein.	☑	☐
4. If you're too thin, you might get sick easily.	☑	☐

B *Group work* Talk about these questions.

1. Which of the tips in the article do you already follow?
2. What do you eat in a typical day? Is your diet balanced? What do you need to eat more of? less of?
3. Can you think of a time when eating (or not eating) affected your performance? What happened?

Review of Units 1–4

1 HOW TIMES HAVE CHANGED!

A ***Group work*** Talk about how family life has changed in the last fifty years in your country. Ask and answer questions like these:

How big were families fifty years ago?
What kinds of homes did people live in then?
What kinds of jobs did men use to have?
And what about women?
How were schools different?
How much did people use to earn?
What kinds of machines and appliances did people use?

B ***Class activity*** Compare answers. Do you think life was better in the old days? Why or why not?

2 CITY PLANNERS

A ***Pair work*** How would you make your city or town a better place for young people? Make suggestions.

A: How would you make the city better for young people?
B: Well, there should be more free concerts in the summer.
A: You're right. And there aren't enough parks.

B ***Group work*** Compare your ideas. Which suggestions do you think are best?

3 LISTENING

Listen to people ask for information. Check (✓) the correct response.

1. ☐ It's just around the corner.
   ☐ Yes, it closes at three.
2. ☐ Yes, it does.
   ☐ The next one is in ten minutes.
3. ☐ On the corner of Main and 15th.
   ☐ At nine o'clock in the morning.
4. ☐ It's in the shopping center on King Street.
   ☐ Not until two o'clock.
5. ☐ Yes, in the Fairmont Hotel on Main Street.
   ☐ Yes, I do.
6. ☐ By bus.
   ☐ On the corner of Orange and Dewey.

4 *COMPUTER SHOPPING*

Pair work Look at these ads for computers. Make comparisons using *as . . . as*. Which computer would you buy?

"Computer 2 isn't as old as computer 1."

For sale: Used IBM computer (4 yrs old). 8 MB of memory. 13 inch screen. $2000. Price includes three software programs. **Call 638-2825.**

FOR SALE:
Used IBM computer (2 yrs old). 16 MB of memory. 20 inch screen. $2000. Price includes two software programs. **Call 638-7693.**

5 *HOME IMPROVEMENTS*

A Make a list of five things you wish you could change about your house or apartment.

B **Pair work** Compare your lists. Give at least one reason for each wish.

A: I wish I had a bigger bedroom.
It's too small for all my things.
B: I know what you mean.
I wish . . . .

6 *TALKING ABOUT FOOD*

A Complete the sentences with information about food.

1. I have never tried .... food.
2. I have tried .... food, but I don't really like it.
3. The most unusual thing I have ever eaten is ....
4. The worst food I have ever tried is ....
5. A dish I have never tried but would like to try is ....
6. I have often cooked ....

B **Pair work** Compare sentences with a partner. Ask and answer follow-up questions.

A: I've never tried Russian food.
B: Oh, I have. It's delicious.
A: What is a common Russian dish?

C **Pair work** Describe how to make a food that you like to cook.

"I like to cook . . . . To make it, first you . . . .
Then . . . . Next, ..."

5 Going places

1 SNAPSHOT

what people like to do on vacation
Discover something new
take language, cooking, or sailing lessons
join an archaeological dig
Enjoy nature
go camping, hiking, or fishing
relax at the beach
Take an exciting trip
visit a foreign country
travel through their own country by car or train
Stay home
catch up on reading
fix up or redecorate the house

Based on information from *U.S. News and World Report* and *American Demographics*

Complete these tasks.

Which of the activities above do you like to do on vacation? Check (✓) the activities.
Make a list of other activities you like to do on vacation. Then compare with a partner.

2 CONVERSATION

A Listen and practice

Julia: I'm so excited! We have two weeks off! What are you going to do?

Nancy: I'm not sure. I guess I'll just stay home. Maybe I'll catch up on my reading. What about you? Any plans?

Julia: Well, my parents have rented a condominium in Florida. I'm going to take long walks along the beach every day and do lots of swimming.

Nancy: Sounds great!

Julia: Say, why don't you come with us? We have plenty of room.

Nancy: Do you mean it? I'd love to!

B ***Class activity*** Have you ever taken a vacation at the beach? What kinds of things can you do there?

3 GRAMMAR FOCUS

Future with be going to *and* will

Use **be going to** *+ verb to talk about plans you've decided on. Use* **will** *+ verb with* **maybe, probably, I guess,** *or* **I think** *to talk about possible plans before you've made a decision.*

Where **are** you **going to go?**	I'**m going to go** to the beach.	I'm not sure. **Maybe I'll catch up** on my reading.
	I'**m** not **going to take** a vacation.	**I probably won't take** a vacation this year.
What **are** you **going to do?**	I'**m going to do** lots of swimming.	**I guess** I'll just **stay** home. I don't know. **I think I'll go** camping.

A Complete the conversation with appropriate forms of *be going to* or *will*. Then compare with a partner.

A: Have you made any vacation plans?
B: Well, I've decided on one thing –
I .... go camping.
A: That's great! For how long?
B: I .... be away for a week.
I only have five days of vacation.
A: So, when are you leaving?
B: I'm not sure. I .... probably leave
around the end of May.
A: And where .... you .... go?
B: I haven't thought about that yet. I guess
I .... go to one of the national parks.
A: That sounds like fun.
B: Yeah. Maybe I .... go
hiking and do some fishing.
A: .... you .... rent a camper?
B: I'm not sure. Actually, I probably ....
rent a camper – it's too expensive.
A: .... you .... go with anyone?
B: No. I need some time alone.
I .... travel by myself.

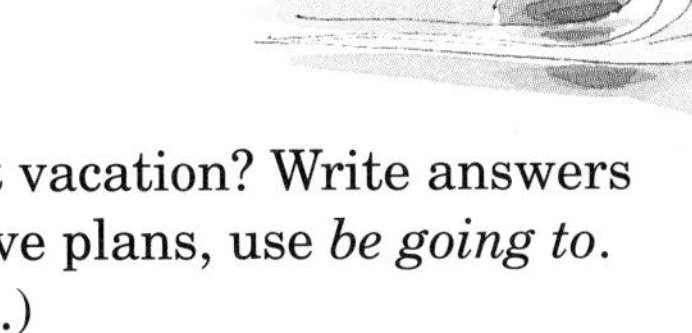

B Have you thought about your next vacation? Write answers to these questions. (If you already have plans, use *be going to*. If you don't have fixed plans, use *will*.)

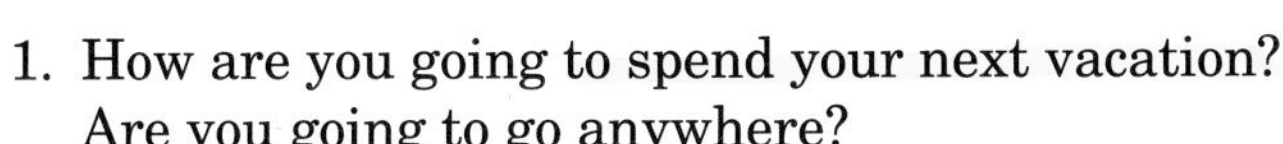

1. How are you going to spend your next vacation? Are you going to go anywhere?
2. When are you going to take your vacation?
3. How long are you going to be on vacation?
4. What are you going to do?
5. Is anyone going to travel with you?

I'm going to take my next vacation . . . .
OR
I'm not sure. Maybe I'll . . . .

C ***Group work*** Take turns telling the group about your vacation plans. Use the information you wrote in part B.

4 WRITING *Itineraries*

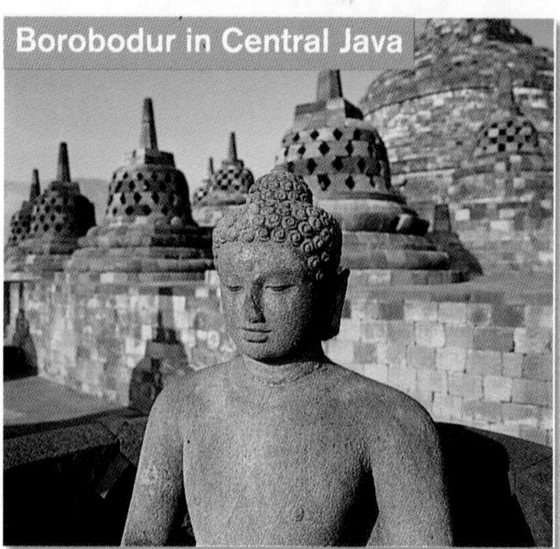
Borobodur in Central Java

Write about the trip you planned in Exercise 3 or another trip you are going to take.

Next summer, I'm going to travel to Indonesia with my family. We're going to visit Borobodur in Central Java. It's one of the biggest temples in the world. And we'll probably visit several other temples nearby. . . .

5 LISTENING

CLASS AUDIO ONLY

A Listen to Judy, Paul, and Brenda describe their summer plans. Check (✓) the correct piece of information about each person's plans.

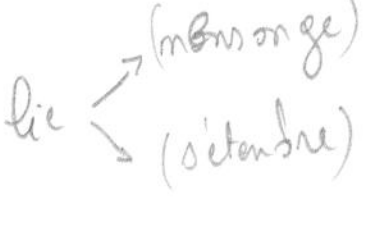

Who . . . ?	1. Judy	2. Paul	3. Brenda
is going to learn about a different culture	☐	☐	☐
will probably visit several different countries	☐	☐	☒
probably won't take a vacation	☐	☒	☐
is going to lie on the beach	☐	☐	☐
is going to do something exciting and a little dangerous	☒	☐	☐

CLASS AUDIO ONLY

B  Listen again. What is the main reason for each person's choice?

6 WORD POWER *Travel*

A Complete the chart. Then add one more word to each category.

backpack
cash
credit card
first-aid kit
hiking boots
medication
overnight bag
passport
plane ticket
shorts
suitcase
traveler's checks
vaccination
visa
windbreaker

Clothing	Money	Health	Travel documents	Luggage
hiking boots	cash	medication	visa	back pack
shorts	credit card	vaccination	passeport	suitcase
windbreaker	traveler's checks	first-aid kit	plane ticket	overnight bag

B ***Pair work*** What are the five most important items you need for these vacations: a trip to a foreign country? a rafting trip? a mountain-climbing expedition?

7 CONVERSATION

A Listen and practice.

Lucy: Hey, Mom. I want to backpack around Europe this summer. What do you think?
Mom: Backpack around Europe? That sounds dangerous! You shouldn't go by yourself. You ought to go with someone.
Lucy: Yes, I've thought of that.
Mom: And you'd better talk to your father first.
Lucy: I already did. He thinks it's a great idea. He wants to come with me!

B *Class activity* Would you like to backpack around Europe? Which countries would you like to visit? Why?

8 GRAMMAR FOCUS

Modals for necessity and suggestion

Describing necessity	*Giving suggestions*
You **have to** get a passport.	You**'d better** talk to your father.
You **must** get a visa for some countries.	You **ought to** go with someone.
You **need to** take money.	You **should** take warm clothes.
For some countries, you **don't have to** get any vaccinations.	You **shouldn't** go by yourself.

A Give advice to someone who is thinking of taking a vacation abroad. Then compare with a partner.

"You must get a passport."
"You shouldn't pack too many clothes."

1. . . . get a passport.
2. . . . pack too many clothes.
3. . . . buy a round-trip plane ticket.
4. . . . make hotel reservations.
5. . . . get a vaccination.
6. . . . check the weather.
7. . . . carry lots of cash.
8. . . . get traveler's checks.
9. . . . take a lot of luggage.
10. . . . check on visas.
11. . . . carry your wallet in your back pocket.
12. . . . take identification with you.

B *Group work* Give four more pieces of advice.

9 PRONUNCIATION Ought to *and* have to

A Listen and practice. Notice the pronunciation of **ought to** and **have to** in these sentences.

You **ought to** take a credit card.
You **ought to** go in June.

You **have to** get a passport.
You **have to** get a visa.

B *Pair work* Write two sentences using *ought to* and two sentences using *have to*. Then practice them with a partner. Pay attention to pronunciation.

10 DREAM VACATION

A *Pair work* You won some money in a lottery. Plan an interesting trip around the world. Discuss these questions and others of your own. Make notes.

Where are we going to start from?
What time of the year should we travel?
How are we going to travel?
What countries and cities should we visit?
How long should we spend in each place?
Where are we going to stay?
What are we planning to do and see there?
How much money do we have to take?
What do we need to take with us?

B *Group work* Compare your plans. Which trip sounds the most exciting?

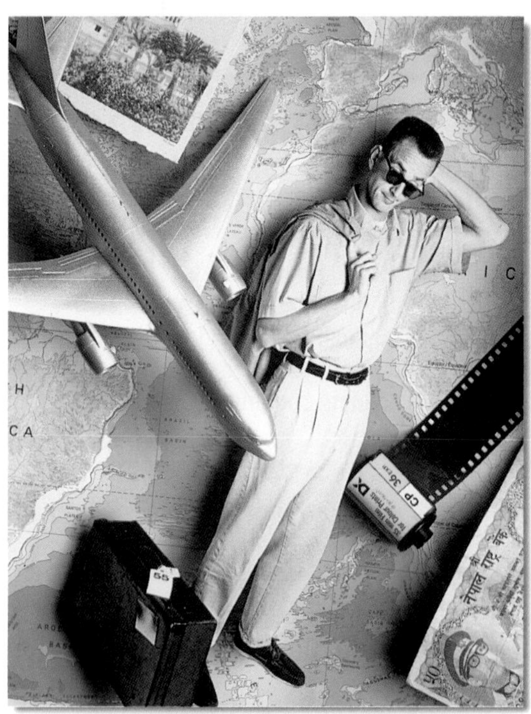

11 LISTENING Tourist tips

A spokesperson from the New York City Visitors and Convention Bureau is giving advice to visitors. What are four things people should do to make their visit to New York City safe and pleasant?

Advice
1. plane your visit before
2. be in a group
3. don't be affraid to ask help for direction
4. don't leave anythink precious in the car

interchange 5

Fun vacations

Decide between two vacations. Student A turns to page IC-6. Student B turns to page IC-8.

12 READING

Getting more for less when you travel

Do you know how to get inexpensive airline and train tickets? hotel accommodations?

On a recent flight, Laura was chatting happily with the woman in the next seat – until the conversation turned to fares. The woman, who bought her ticket two months in advance, paid $109. Laura paid the full fare of $457. She decided that next time she would find out how to travel for less.

Here are some ways to travel for less:

traveling by train in Europe

Cheap airplane tickets. To fly for less money, you can buy non-refundable plane tickets two or three months before your trip. The cheapest way to fly is as a courier. In return for delivering a package for a courier company, you get a plane ticket that costs as little as one-quarter of the regular fare – or even less if the company needs someone at the last minute. Recently, a courier flew round trip from Los Angeles to Tokyo for $100; a regular ticket cost around $1,800.

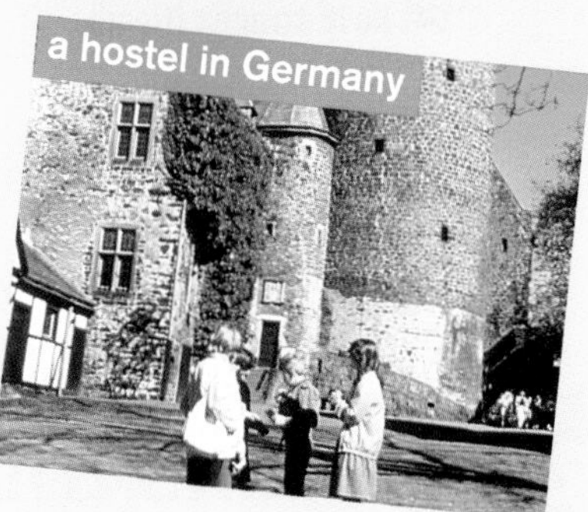

a hostel in Germany

Train passes. If you're going to do a lot of traveling by train, a train pass will save you money. Buying a single pass gives you unlimited travel for a period of time. Train passes can be especially useful in India, which has the world's largest rail system; in Japan, where trains are fast and convenient; and in Europe, where trains go to over 30,000 cities.

Hostels. Hostels used to provide cheap accommodations – in dormitories – for people under the age of 25. Nowadays, hostels don't have any age requirements. They're not only cheap ($8–$17 a night) but a great way to meet people. Hostels are often in interesting places – a castle in Germany, a lighthouse in California, a one-room schoolhouse in the wilderness of Australia. And sometimes hostels have luxuries like swimming pools.

A In your own words, restate some of the information from the article using the phrases below.

1. 25% of the normal fare — *"Fly as a courier. You can buy your plane ticket for one-quarter of the normal fare."*
2. $100 instead of $1,800
3. more than 30,000 cities
4. younger than 25
5. $17 or less

B ***Pair work*** Talk about these questions. Give reasons for your answers.

1. Would you want to travel as an air courier? take a long train trip? stay in a hostel?
2. What advice would you give someone who wants to travel for less in your country? Which hotels, restaurants, means of transportation, and stores would you recommend?

6 Sure. No problem!

1 SNAPSHOT

Common complaints of families with teenagers

Parents about teens:

My kids . . .

- don't help around the house.
- don't listen to my advice.
- have strange friends.
- dress badly and have ugly hairstyles.
- watch too much TV.
- don't study enough.

Teens about parents:

My parents . . .

- nag about chores and homework.
- don't like my friends.
- criticize my appearance.
- don't respect my privacy.
- always tell me what to do.
- don't listen to my opinions.

Based on information from America Online's Parent Resource Site

Talk about these questions.

Have you ever heard parents or children make these complaints? Which ones?
Have you ever had any complaints like these about family members?

2 CONVERSATION *Making requests*

A Listen and practice.

Mr. Field: Jason . . . Jason! Turn down the TV a little, please.
Jason: Oh, but this is my favorite program!
Mr. Field: I know. But it's very loud.
Jason: OK. I'll turn it down.
Mr. Field: That's better. Thanks.
Mrs. Field: Lisa, please pick up your things. They're all over the living room floor.
Lisa: In a minute, Mom. I'm on the phone.
Mrs. Field: OK. But do it as soon as you hang up.
Lisa: Sure. No problem!
Mrs. Field: Goodness! Were we like this when we were kids?
Mr. Field: Definitely!

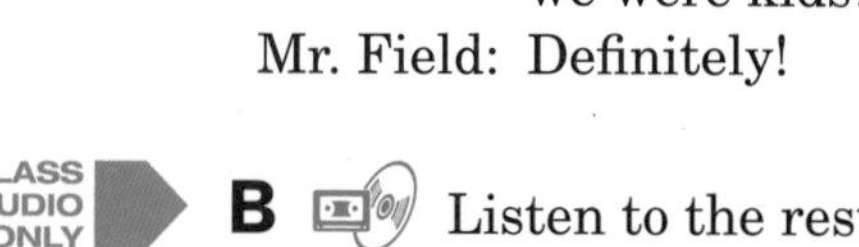

CLASS AUDIO ONLY

B Listen to the rest of the conversation. What complaints do Jason and Lisa have about their parents?

3 GRAMMAR FOCUS

Two-part verbs; *will* for responding to requests

With nouns	*With pronouns*	*Requests and responses*
Turn down the TV. **Turn** the TV **down**.	**Turn** it **down**.	Please turn down the music. OK. I'**ll** turn it down.
Pick up your things. **Pick** your things **up**.	**Pick** them **up**.	Pick up your clothes, please. Sure. I'**ll** pick them up.

A Complete the requests with these words. Then compare with a partner.

the books | the toys | the radio | your coat | the TV

your boots | the yard | the light | the trash | your cigarette

1. Pick up *the toys*, please.
2. Turn .... off, please.
3. Clean .... up, please.
4. Please put .... away.
5. Please turn down ....
6. Please take off ....
7. Hang .... up, please.
8. Please take out ....
9. Please put .... out.
10. Turn on .... , please.

B *Pair work* Take turns making the requests above. Respond with pronouns.

A: Pick up the toys, please.
B: Sure. I'll pick them up.

4 PRONUNCIATION *Stress with two-part verbs*

A Listen and practice. Both words in a two-part verb receive equal stress.

Please **túrn dówn** the radio.	**Túrn** it **dówn**.
Píck the magazines **úp**, please.	**Píck** them **úp**.

B Write four more requests using the verbs in Exercise 3. Then practice with a partner. Pay attention to stress.

5 WORD POWER *Household chores*

A Find a phrase in the list that is usually paired with each verb. (Some phrases go with more than one verb.) Can you think of one more phrase for each verb?

the counter	the cat	the dry cleaning	the faucet	the groceries
the mess	the oven	the garbage	the newspapers	the towels

clean off	....	....	put out	....	....
clean up	....	....	take out	....	....
hang up	....	....	throw out	....	....
pick up	....	....	turn off	....	....
put away	....	....	turn on	....	....

B What requests can you make in each of these places?
Write four requests and four unusual excuses. Use two-part verbs.

the kitchen	the living room
the bathroom	the bedroom

C ***Pair work*** Take turns making the requests you wrote in part B. Respond by giving an unusual excuse.

A: Mark, please clean up your mess in the kitchen.
B: I can't clean it up right now. I have to take the cat out for a walk.

6 LISTENING *Excuses, excuses!*

A Listen to parents ask their children to do things. Match each conversation with the picture it describes. Number the pictures from 1 to 5.

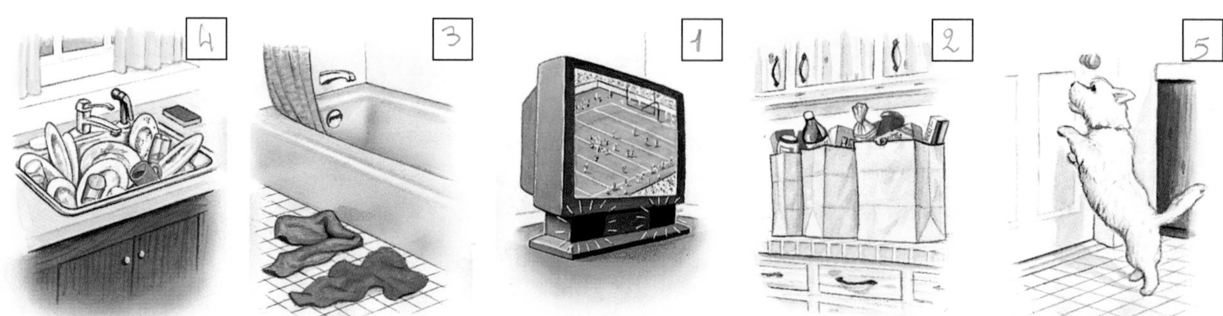

B  Listen again. What excuse does each person give?

7 CONVERSATION

A Listen and practice.

George: Hi. I'm your new neighbor, George Rivera. I live next door.
Stephanie: Oh, hi. I'm Stephanie Lee.
George: So, you just moved in? Do you need anything?
Stephanie: Not right now. But thanks.
George: Well, let me know if you do. Um, by the way, would you mind turning your stereo down? The walls are really thin, so the sound goes right through to my apartment.
Stephanie: Oh, I'm sorry! I didn't realize that. I'll make sure to keep the volume down. Oh, by the way, is there a good Italian restaurant in the neighborhood?
George: Yeah. There's a great one a couple of blocks from here. Try their lasagna. It's delicious!

B *Pair work* Has a situation like the one in part A ever happened to you? What did you do?

8 APOLOGIES

People apologize in different ways.
For example, if someone complains about the noise from your stereo, you can:

apologize and . . .	**give an excuse**	"I'm sorry. I didn't realize."
	admit a mistake	"I forgot I left it on."
	make an offer	"I'll turn it down right now."
	make a promise	"I'll make sure to keep the volume down."

People often apologize in more than one way. For example, in Exercise 7, Stephanie apologized, gave an excuse, and made a promise.

A *Class activity* How do people usually apologize in your country? What do you usually do when you apologize?

B Listen to three people complaining. What are they complaining about? How does the other person apologize? (More than one answer is possible.)

Complaint	Type of apology			
	give an excuse	admit a mistake	make an offer	make a promise
1.	☐	☐	☐	☐
2.	☐	☐	☐	☐
3.	☐	☐	☐	☐

9 GRAMMAR FOCUS

Requests with modals and Would you mind . . . ?

Modal + simple form of verb	*Would you mind . . . ? + gerund*
Can you **turn** the stereo **down**?	**Would** you **mind turning** the stereo **down**?
Could you **leave** the door open, please?	**Would** you **mind not closing** the door, please?
Would you please **keep** the noise down?	**Would** you **mind keeping** the noise down?

A Match the requests with the appropriate responses. Then compare with a partner and practice them. (More than one answer may be possible.)

1. Could you lend me twenty dollars? ......
2. Would you mind picking up a sandwich for me? ......
3. Can you help me move into my new apartment tomorrow? ......
4. Would you mind not smoking here? ......
5. Would you please move your car? It's blocking my driveway. ......
6. Would you mind not talking so loud? ......

a. We're sorry. We'll talk more quietly.
b. Sorry. I'll do it right away.
c. Oh, I'm sorry. I didn't realize this was the non-smoking section.
d. Are you kidding? I'm totally broke!
e. I'm really sorry, but I'm busy.
f. Sure, no problem. I'd be glad to.

"I'm totally broke!"

B ***Pair work*** Take turns making the requests in part A. This time give your own responses.

C ***Class activity*** Think of five unusual requests. Go around the class and make your requests. How many people accepted and how many refused?

10 WRITING

A Write a letter to a "rich relative," asking him or her to lend you some money. Explain why you need it and when you will pay it back.

Dear Uncle John,
I'm planning to drive across the U.S. by car when I graduate. The only problem is, I can't afford to buy a car. Would you mind lending me $4,000 to help me buy one? I'll pay you back as soon as I get a job. . . .

That's no excuse!

How good are you at apologizing? Turn to page IC-7.

B ***Pair work*** Exchange letters with a partner. Write a reply to your partner's request.

11 READING

Summer in the Country

How is summer in the country different for young people from summer in the city?

a Fresh Air Fund camp

"Before I came here," one child said, "I thought swimming was running through an open fire hydrant."

"Here" is a summer camp that's only an hour from New York City – but a world away. This camp and four others nearby are run by the Fresh Air Fund. Since 1877, the fund has helped poor children from New York City spend summers in the country. Each year, over ten thousand children, ages 6 to 18, participate in the program. Some stay at a camp; others live with a host family. The fund pays for all expenses.

The camps are for 8- to 15-year-olds. At camp, children can learn about the stars, see deer and cows and other animals, and go hiking, fishing, and of course, swimming. The children learn responsibility by helping out with chores like making beds and waiting on tables. They also learn a lot from counselors, who are often college students from around the United States and from other countries.

summer in New York City

Host families from thirteen states and Canada volunteer to have children spend the summer with them. Many of these families have their own children. The visiting children become part of the family. They go with the family on picnics, to the pool or beach, and on trips. The children are from 6 to 12 years old when they make their first visit, and most are invited back. Some of the children and families become friends for life.

A Read the article. Imagine you work for the Fresh Air Fund. A mother wants to send her child and calls to ask for information. How would you answer these questions?

1. Is the Fresh Air Fund program new?
2. Are the camps far from New York City?
3. What are some things children do at camp?
4. Does the Fresh Air Fund run only summer camps?
5. Can a 7-year-old go to camp?
6. Can a 7-year-old live with a host family?
7. What are some things children do with host families?
8. Can a child who lives with a host family go back for a second year?

B *Pair work* Talk about these questions. Give reasons for your answers.

1. If you were a child in New York City, would you rather go to a camp or live with a host family?
2. Would you like to be a counselor at a Fresh Air Fund camp?
3. How does the Fresh Air Fund benefit children? host families?

7 What's this for?

1 SNAPSHOT

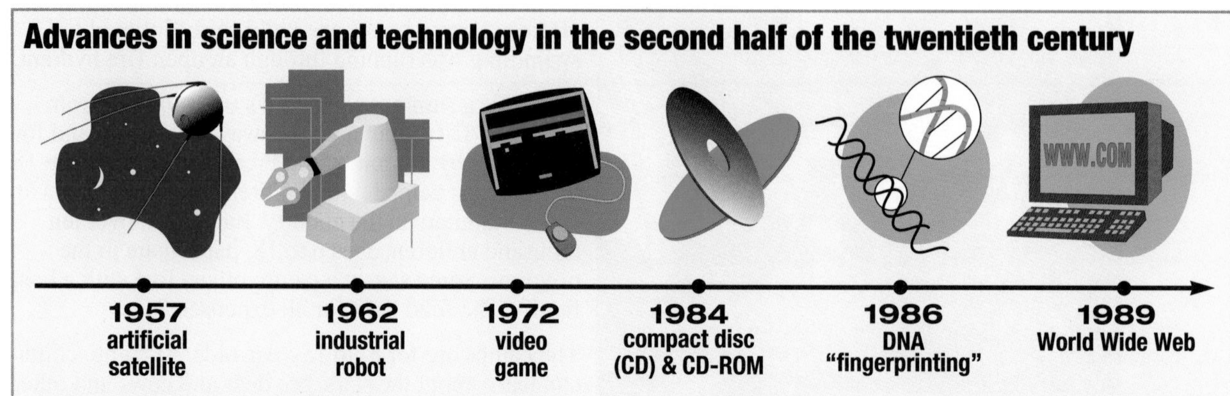

Sources: *The Universal Almanac, The New York Public Library Source Desk Reference*

Talk about these questions.

Can you explain the significance of each of these advances? Which do you think is the most important? the least important?
Which have affected your life? Which have not?

2 CONVERSATION

A Listen and practice.

Daniel: Hey! Nice computer! What's this for?
Andrea: That's a modem. It's used to connect the computer to the phone line, so I can send faxes and access the Internet.
Daniel: So you can go on-line and all that?
Andrea: Yes. And I use the World Wide Web for finding information on astronomy, movies, UFOs – just about anything.
Daniel: Sports? Cars?
Andrea: Uh-huh. And I can exchange information with people, too. I belong to a "chat group" on astronomy.
Daniel: Hmm. I just use my computer to write letters and reports.
Andrea: Why don't you get on the Internet? It's not really expensive.
Daniel: Maybe I will. It sounds like fun.

B Listen to the rest of the conversation. What else does Andrea use her computer for?

3 GRAMMAR FOCUS

Infinitives and gerunds

Infinitives and gerunds can describe a use or a purpose.

Infinitives	*Gerunds*
A modem is used **to connect** computers to phones.	It's used **for connecting** computers to phones.
Computers are often used **to write** letters.	They're often used **for writing** letters.
I can use the World Wide Web **to find** information.	I can use it **for finding** information.

A What do you know about this technology? Complete the phrases in column A with information from column B. Then compare with a partner. (More than one answer is possible.)

A	*B*
1. Satellites are used . . .	study the world's weather
2. Robots are sometimes used . . .	perform dangerous tasks
3. You can use a fax machine . . .	read the latest weather report
4. People use the Internet . . .	transmit telephone calls
5. DNA fingerprinting is used . . .	make a photocopy
6. CD-ROM is sometimes used . . .	identify criminals
	make travel reservations
	transmit television programs
	store an encyclopedia

Satellites are used for transmitting telephone calls.
Satellites are used to transmit telephone calls.

B *Group work* Take turns completing the phrases in column A with your own information.

4 PRONUNCIATION *Syllable stress*

A Where is the stress in these words and compound nouns? Mark the stressed syllable. Then listen and check.

television programs	travel reservations	fingerprinting	fax machine
telephone calls	weather report	photocopy	Internet

B *Pair work* Practice the statements you wrote in Exercise 3. Pay attention to syllable stress.

5 WORD POWER *The world of computers*

A What are three uses for computers at home? at school? in a factory? in a restaurant? Complete the chart. Then add two more uses for each place.

communicate with people	create the menu	create work schedules
keep the attendance	make budgets	make report cards
pay household bills	pay the workers	place orders
process credit cards	research papers	run the machines

At home	At school	In a factory	In a restaurant
....	....	....	....
....	....	....	....
....	....	....	....
....	....	....	....
....	....	....	....

B ***Group work*** Compare your lists with classmates. Talk about the different uses for computers.

A: At home, people use computers to pay household bills.
B: My mother uses ours for making budgets.
C: I use mine to communicate with people on the Internet.

6 LISTENING

A ***Pair work*** How do you think these people use computers in their work? Make two guesses.

Sandy Watson is a police officer. She analyzes crime patterns.

to follow up information

Alex Hunt is a psychotherapist. He helps people change their behaviors.

to categorate their behavior

Janet Brown is a professor. She teaches at a medical school.

to make progress report

B Listen to interviews with the people in part A. Were your guesses correct?

7 CONVERSATION

A Listen and practice.

Jennifer: I read the instructions, but I'm still not sure how to use my cellular phone.
Richard: Actually, it's pretty easy. First of all, don't forget to turn it on.
Jennifer: Got it!
Richard: Then dial the number. And remember to press the "send" button.
Jennifer: That's all?
Richard: Pretty much. Just make sure to recharge the batteries every few weeks. And try not to drop it. It's fragile.
Jennifer: Good advice.
Richard: And one more thing: Be sure to pay the phone bill every month!

B *Class activity* How many advantages can you think of for owning a cellular phone?

8 GRAMMAR FOCUS

Infinitive complements

Don't forget to turn it on.
Remember to press the "send" button.
Make sure to recharge the batteries.
Try not to drop it.
Be sure to pay the phone bill every month.

A Look at these pieces of advice. Which ones refer to a microwave oven (**M**)? a hair dryer (**H**)? a laptop computer (**L**)? (More than one answer is possible.) Then think of another piece of advice for each thing.

1. Unplug it after you use it. ....
2. Save your work often. ....
3. Recharge the batteries often. ....
4. Keep it away from water. ....
5. Don't spill drinks on it. ....
6. Don't put metal in it. ....
7. Don't heat closed containers in it. ....
8. Don't expose it to extreme heat or cold. ....

B *Pair work* Take turns giving advice for using the items above. Use these phrases.

Don't forget to	Try to	Make sure to . . . .
Remember to	Try not to	Be sure not to . . . .

9 FREE ADVICE

A Listen to people give advice about three of the things below. Write down the name of each item.

fax machine

motorbike

camcorder

in-line skates

ATM card

personal watercraft

	Item	Advice
1.	....	....
2.	....	....
3.	....	....

B Listen again. Complete the chart with a piece of advice for each item. Then compare answers with classmates.

C ***Group work*** What do you know about the other items in the pictures? What advice would you give to someone about them?

"With a fax machine, remember to put the document facedown."

Good advice

Do you give good advice? Student A turns to page IC-9. Student B turns to page IC-10.

10 WRITING

Choose a useful item that you own. Imagine you're going to lend it to a friend. Write a paragraph giving advice on how to use it.

It's easy to use my fax machine. First, plug it into an electrical outlet. Then connect it to a phone line and turn it on. Remember to put the document facedown. Then dial the person's number. . . .

11 READING

A Day in Your Life – In the Year 2020

What are two ways that technology will probably change your life in the next 20–25 years?

People used to know more or less how their children would live. Now things are changing so quickly that we don't even know what our own lives will be like in a few years. What follows is not science fiction. It's how experts see the future.

You're daydreaming behind the wheel of your car, but that's OK. You have it on automatic pilot, and with its high-tech computers and cameras, your car "knows" how to get you home safely.

You're hungry, so you head for the kitchen as soon as you get home. You ordered groceries by computer an hour ago, and you know that by now they've arrived. Your kitchen has a two-way refrigerator, which opens to the outside to accept deliveries. You've already paid for the food by having the money subtracted from your bank account. Nobody uses cash anymore.

What's for lunch? In the old days, you used to stop off to buy a hamburger or pizza. Now you use your diagnostic machine to find out which foods your body needs. You find out you need more vegetables and less fat. Your food-preparation machine makes you a salad.

After lunch, you go down the hall to your home office. Here you have everything you need for doing your work. Thanks to your information screen and your new computer, you almost never go into the office anymore.

The information screen shows an urgent message from a co-worker in Brazil. You set the screen to translate Portuguese into English. As you wait, you think about later, when you'll have a movie transmitted. What movie should you order tonight?

A ***Class activity*** In your own words, tell about a change mentioned in the reading in each of these areas.

1. transportation
2. food
3. money
4. work
5. communications
6. entertainment

B ***Pair work*** Talk about these questions. Give reasons for your answers.

1. Which of the changes sounds the most interesting and useful? Are there any changes that you don't like?
2. Imagine you could invent a machine that would make life easier and better. Describe the machine.

8 Let's celebrate!

1 SNAPSHOT

Holidays and Festivals
Chinese New Year
January or February
Chinese people celebrate with firecrackers and lion dances.
Valentine's Day
February 14
People in many countries give chocolates, flowers, or jewelry to the person they love.
Children's Day (formerly Boys' Day)
May 5
Japanese families put up colored streamers shaped like fish, in honor of their children.
Day of the Dead
November 2
Mexican families offer food to the dead and then have a meal in a cemetery.
Thanksgiving
Fall
In October in Canada and in November in the United States, people celebrate the harvest by preparing a large meal. They usually serve roast turkey.

Source: *Reader's Digest Book of Facts*

Talk about these questions.

Do you have holidays similar to these in your country?
What other special days do you have? What's your favorite holiday or festival?

2 WORD POWER *Celebrations*

Pair work Complete the word map. Add two more words to each category. Then compare with a partner

anniversary
cake
cards
champagne
dancing
fireworks
flowers
parade
party
presents
roast turkey
wedding

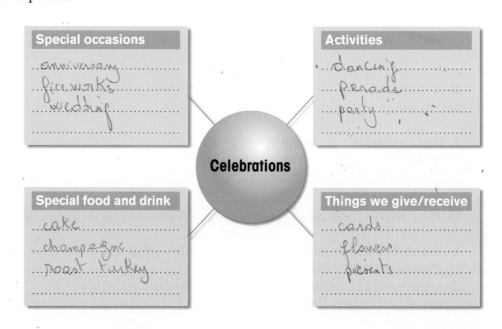

Celebrations

Special occasions
anniversary
fireworks
wedding

Activities
dancing
parade
party

Special food and drink
cake
champagne
roast turkey

Things we give/receive
cards
flowers
presents

3 CONVERSATION

A Listen and practice.

Leo: Did you know next week is Halloween? It's on October 31.
Natasha: So what do you do on Halloween? We don't have that holiday in Russia.
Leo: Well, it's a day when kids dress up in masks and costumes. They knock on people's doors and ask for candy by saying the words "Trick or treat!"
Natasha: Hmm. Sounds interesting.
Leo: But it's not just for kids. Lots of people have costume parties. Hey . . . my friend Pete is having a party. Would you like to go?
Natasha: Sure. I'd love to.

B Listen to the rest of the conversation. What are Leo and Natasha going to wear to the Halloween party?

4 GRAMMAR FOCUS

Relative clauses of time

Halloween is **a day when kids in the United States dress up in masks and costumes.**
November 2 is **the day when Mexicans observe the Day of the Dead.**
Fall is **the season when people in the United States and Canada celebrate Thanksgiving.**

A How much do you know about these days and months? Complete the sentences in column A with information from column B. Then compare with a partner.

A	B
1. New Year's Eve is a night when ...b...	a. Brazilians celebrate Carnival.
2. April Fools' Day is a day when ..d...	b. people like to "party."
3. May Day is a day when ....e..	c. the French celebrate their revolution.
4. Valentine's Day is a day when .F.....	d. people play tricks on friends.
5. July 14 is the day when ..c....	e. people in many countries honor workers.
6. February is the month when ....a..	f. people give presents to the ones they love.

B Complete these sentences with information of your own. Then compare with a partner.

1. Winter is a season .when we can do ski
2. Spring is a time of the year .when flowers emerge from the soil
3. Mother's Day is the day .when people give presents to their mother
4. A birthday is a day .when we celebrate our birth
5. A wedding anniversary is a time .when we celebrate a wedding day

5 LISTENING

Mike has just returned from Brazil. Listen to him talk about Carnival. Take notes to answer these questions.

What is Carnival? street party
How long does it last? 4 days
When is it? late February, begin march
What is the best part about it? a big parade
What is the samba? special dance

Carnival in Brazil

6 ONCE A YEAR

A ***Pair work*** Take turns asking and answering these questions and others of your own.

What's the most interesting holiday or festival in your country?
When is it?
How do people celebrate it?
Do you eat any special food?
What do you like most about it?
What else do people do?

B ***Class activity*** Give a short talk about an interesting holiday or festival. Answer any questions your classmates may have.

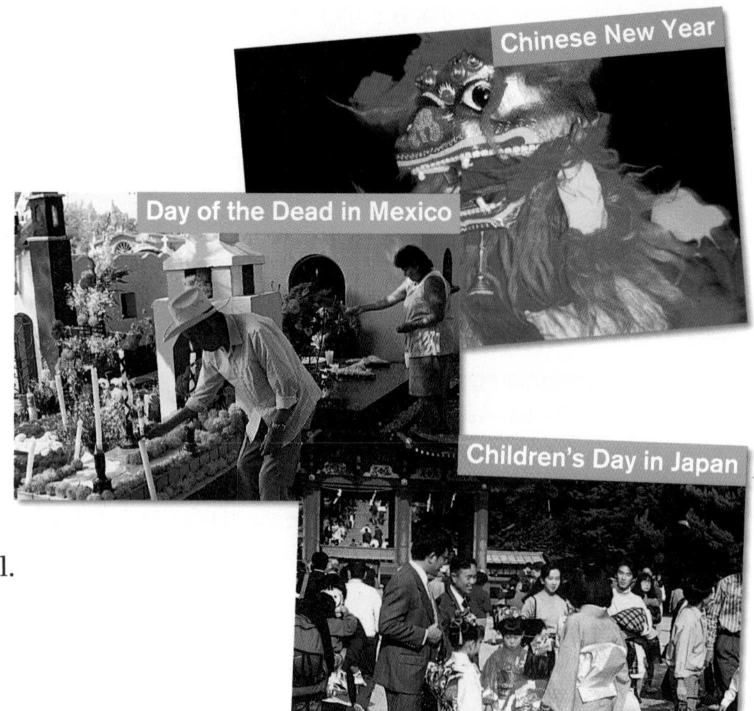
Chinese New Year
Day of the Dead in Mexico
Children's Day in Japan

7 WRITING

A Write about your favorite holiday or festival. What usually happens? What do you usually do?

My favorite holiday is Thanksgiving. In the United States, it's always the fourth Thursday in November. Everyone in my family gets together at my parents' house. We cook a large turkey and serve it with cranberry sauce. . . .

B ***Pair work*** Read your partner's composition. Do you have any questions?

8 CONVERSATION

A Listen and practice.

Jill: You look beautiful in that kimono, Mari. Is this your wedding photo?
Mari: Yes, it is.
Jill: Do most Japanese women wear kimonos when they get married?
Mari: Yes, many of them do. Then after the wedding ceremony, the bride usually changes into a Western bridal dress during the reception.
Jill: Oh, I didn't know that.

CLASS AUDIO ONLY

B Listen to the rest of the conversation. Take notes to answer these questions.

Where was Mari's wedding held?
Who attended the wedding ceremony?
What happened at the reception?

9 PRONUNCIATION Stress and rhythm

A Listen and practice. The words with the most important information in a sentence are usually stressed.

When **wó**men get **már**ried in Ja**pán**, they **ú**su**ally** **wéar** ki**mó**nos.
After the **wéd**ding **cé**remony, they **chánge** into **Wés**tern **clóthes**.

B *Pair work* Mark the stress in these sentences. Listen and check. Then practice the sentences.

Halloween is a day when children go "trick-or-treating."
On Thanksgiving Day, Americans eat turkey and cranberry sauce.
When people have birthdays, they usually get presents from friends.
June is a month when many young people like to get married.

10 GRAMMAR FOCUS

Adverbial clauses of time

Before a Japanese couple gets married, they send wedding announcements.
When they get married, they usually wear kimonos.
After they return from the honeymoon, they move into their own home.

A Read this information about marriages in North America. Match the clauses in column A with information from column B.

A

1. Before a man and a woman get married, ...
2. Before the man gets married, ...
3. When the woman gets engaged, ...
4. When the woman gets married, ...
5. After the couple gets married, ...
6. After they return from their honeymoon, ...

B

a. the newlyweds usually live on their own.
b. she usually wears a white wedding dress.
c. they usually date each other for a year or so.
d. his male friends often give him a bachelor party.
e. her female friends often give her a bridal shower.
f. there's usually a wedding reception.

B ***Pair work*** What happens when people get married in your country? Add your own information to the clauses in column A. Pay attention to rhythm and stress.

Once in a blue moon
How do your classmates celebrate special events? Turn to page IC-11.

11 MARRIAGE CUSTOMS

Group work Talk about marriage customs in your country. Ask these questions and others of your own.

How old are people usually when they get married?
Is there an engagement period? How long is it?
Who pays for the wedding?
Who is invited?
Where is the wedding ceremony usually held?
What happens during the ceremony?
What do the bride and groom usually wear?
Is there a reception after the ceremony?
What type of food is served at the reception?
What kinds of gifts do people usually give?
Where do couples like to go on their honeymoon?
How long is the honeymoon?

12 READING

Unique customs

Look at the photos below. What do you think is happening in each picture?

January 17 is **St. Anthony's Day** in Mexico. It's a day when people ask for protection for their animals. They bring their animals to church. But before the animals go into the church, the people usually dress them up in flowers and ribbons.

On August 15 of the lunar calendar, Koreans celebrate **Chusok** to give thanks for the harvest. It's a day when people honor their ancestors by going to their graves to take them food and wine and clean the gravesites. Also on Chusok, a big meal with moon-shaped rice cakes is eaten.

One of the biggest celebrations in Argentina is **New Year's Eve**. On the evening of December 31, families get together and have a big meal. At midnight, fireworks explode everywhere and continue throughout the night. Friends and families meet for parties, which last until the next morning.

Long ago in India, a princess who needed help sent her silk bracelet to an emperor. After he helped the princess, the emperor kept the bracelet as a sign of the loyalty between them. Today in India, during the festival of **Rakhi**, men promise to be loyal to their women in exchange for a bracelet of silk, cotton, or gold thread.

On the evening of February 3, people in Japanese families take one dried bean for each year of their age and throw the beans around their homes and shrines, shouting "Good luck in! Evil spirits out!" This is known as **"Setsubun,"** a time to celebrate the end of winter and the beginning of spring.

A Read the article. Make five correct sentences using an item from each column.

A	*B*	*C*
On January 17,	people in Japan	visit the graves of their ancestors.
During Rakhi,	people in Argentina	bring their animals to church.
On Chusok,	men in India	stay up all night.
On New Year's Eve,	people in Mexico	celebrate the end of winter.
On February 3,	people in Korea	promise loyalty to their women.

B ***Pair work*** Is there a holiday or custom in your country that is similar to one described here? Describe the holiday or custom.

Review of Units 5–8

1 RESOLUTIONS

A ***Group work*** What are you planning to do or thinking about doing during the next year? Tell your group about at least three things.

"I'm going to take dancing lessons."
"I'll probably go on a diet."

B ***Class activity*** Tell the class about the most interesting or unusual plans in your group.

A: Bob is going to take dancing lessons.
B: And he thinks he'll go on a diet, too.

2 ON THE ROAD

A ***Group work*** Your friends are planning a long car trip for their next vacation. What plans do they need to make? How many suggestions can you think of? Use *had better, must, ought to, should,* and *shouldn't.*

A: You should take some road maps.
B: You'd better check the tires on your car.
C: You ought to check the oil.

B ***Class activity*** Compare your suggestions around the class.

3 ROLE PLAY *I'm sorry. I'll . . . .*

Student A: Complain to your partner about these things:

Your partner has not returned your tennis racquet.
Your partner is playing a CD loudly. You are trying to study.
Your partner has been using the telephone for almost an hour. You need to make an important call.

Student B: Listen to your partner's complaints.
Apologize and make suitable responses.

Change roles and try the role play again.

4 WONDER GADGET

A ***Group work*** Imagine that this is a popular new gadget. Think of as many possible uses for this item as you can.

A: You can use this gadget for . . . .
B: It's used to . . . .

B ***Class activity*** Tell the class your ideas. Which uses do you think are the most interesting?

5 THAT'S AN INTERESTING CUSTOM.

A ***Group work*** What interesting customs do you know for births, marriages, the seasons, or good luck? Take turns talking about them like this:

"When a boy courts a girl in some parts of the Philippines, he stands outside her house at night and sings to her."

Others ask questions.

Why does he do that?
Is it just a village custom?
Is it common?

B ***Class activity*** Which was the most interesting custom you talked about in your group? Tell the class about it.

6 LISTENING

A Listen to some information about unusual marriage customs. Check (✓) True or False for each statement.

Marriage customs	True	False
1. When two women of a tribe in Paraguay want to marry the same man, they put on boxing gloves and fight it out.	☐	☐
2. When a man and a woman get married in Malaysia, they eat cooked rice the day before the wedding.	☐	☐
3. In Italy, before a man and a woman get married, a friend or relative releases two white doves into the air.	☐	☐
4. In some parts of India, when a man and a woman get married, water is poured over them.	☐	☐

B Listen again. For the statements that you marked false, write the correct information.

Interchange Activities

interchange 1 CLASS PROFILE

A ***Class activity*** Go around the class and find out the information below. Then ask follow-up questions and take notes. Write a classmate's name only once.

I used to look very different.

Find someone who . . .	Name	Notes
1. used to look very different. **"Did you use to look very different?"**	....	....
2. used to have a favorite toy when he or she was a child. **"Did you use to have a favorite toy when you were a child?"**	....	....
3. always listened to his or her teachers. **"Did you always listen to your teachers?"**	....	....
4. hated high school. **"Did you hate high school?"**	....	....
5. used to fight a lot with his or her brothers and sisters. **"Did you use to fight a lot with your brothers and sisters?"**	....	....
6. dated someone for a long time in high school. **"Did you "go steady" with someone in high school?"**	....	....
7. wanted to be a movie star when he or she was younger. **"Did you want to be a movie star when you were younger?"**	....	....
8. had a pet when he or she was a child. **"Did you have a pet when you were a child?"**	....	....

B ***Group work*** Tell the group the most interesting thing you learned about your classmates.

interchange 2 MAKING THE CITY BETTER

A Read this letter to a local newspaper.

Letters to the Editor

Dear Editor:

I am sick and tired of the traffic in this city! It is so bad that I can never get anywhere on time. There are too many cars on the road, and most of them have only one person in them.

Another problem is the buses. They are so old and slow that nobody wants to take them. They are noisy and very dirty. You can't even see out the windows!

Also, the taxi drivers are rude. They never know where they are going, and they take a long time to get someplace. Taxis are expensive, too. And the subway is just too crowded and dangerous. What are we going to do?

George Grady
Oakville

B *Group work* Suggest five ways to solve the transportation problems in Oakville.

"Taxi drivers should take classes to learn how to be friendly."

C *Class activity* Tell your group's ideas to the class. Then decide which suggestions are best.

interchange 3 WISHFUL THINKING

A Complete this questionnaire with information about yourself.

WISH LIST

1. **What kind of vacation do you wish you could take?**
   I wish I . . . .
2. **What sport do you wish you could play?**
   ....
3. **Which country do you wish you could live in?**
   ....
4. **What kind of home do you wish you could have?**
   ....
5. **What kind of pet do you wish you could have?**
   ....
6. **What languages do you wish you could speak?**
   ....
7. **Which musical instrument do you wish you could play?**
   ....
8. **What kind of car do you wish you could buy?**
   ....
9. **What famous people do you wish you could meet?**
   ....
10. **What are two things you wish you could change about yourself?**
    ....

B ***Pair work*** Compare your questionnaires. Take turns asking and answering questions about your wishes.

A: What kind of vacation do you wish you could take?
B: I wish I could go on a safari.
A: Really? Why?
B: Well, I could take some great pictures of wild animals!

C ***Class activity*** Imagine that you are at a class reunion. It is ten years since you completed the questionnaire in part A. Tell the class about some wishes that have come true for your partner.

"Sue is a photographer now. She travels to Africa every year and takes pictures of wild animals. Her photos are in many magazines."

interchange 4 RISKY BUSINESS

A How much do you really know about your classmates?
Look at the survey and add two more situations to items 1 and 2.

	Name	Notes
1. Find someone who has . . .		
a. cried during a movie.	....	....
b. gone for a moonlight swim.	....	....
c. sung in a band.	....	....
d. studied all night for an exam.	....	....
e. lied about his or her age.	....	....
f.	....	....
g.	....	....
2. Find someone who has never . . .		
a. eaten a hot dog.	....	....
b. been on a blind date.	....	....
c. seen a wild animal.	....	....
d. kissed someone in public.	....	....
e. driven a car.	....	....
f.	....	....
g.	....	....

B ***Class activity*** Go around the class and ask the questions in the survey. Write down the names of classmates who answer "Yes" for item 1 and "No" for item 2. Then ask follow-up questions and take notes.

A: Have you ever cried during a movie?
B: Yes. I've cried during a lot of movies.
A: What kinds of movies?
B: Well, sad ones like *Casablanca* and . . . .

A: Have you ever eaten a hot dog?
C: No, I haven't
A: Why not?
C: Well, I'm a vegetarian.

C ***Group work*** Compare the information in your surveys.

interchange 5 FUN VACATIONS

Student A

A ***Pair work*** You and your partner are going to take a trip. You have a brochure for a ski trip, and your partner has a brochure for a surfing trip. First ask questions like these about the surfing trip:

How much does the trip cost?
What does the price of the trip include?
What are the accommodations like?
Are surfing lessons available?
Is there going to be anything else to do? Tell me about the nightlife.
What else can you tell me about the trip?

B ***Pair work*** Now use the information in this brochure to answer your partner's questions about the ski trip.

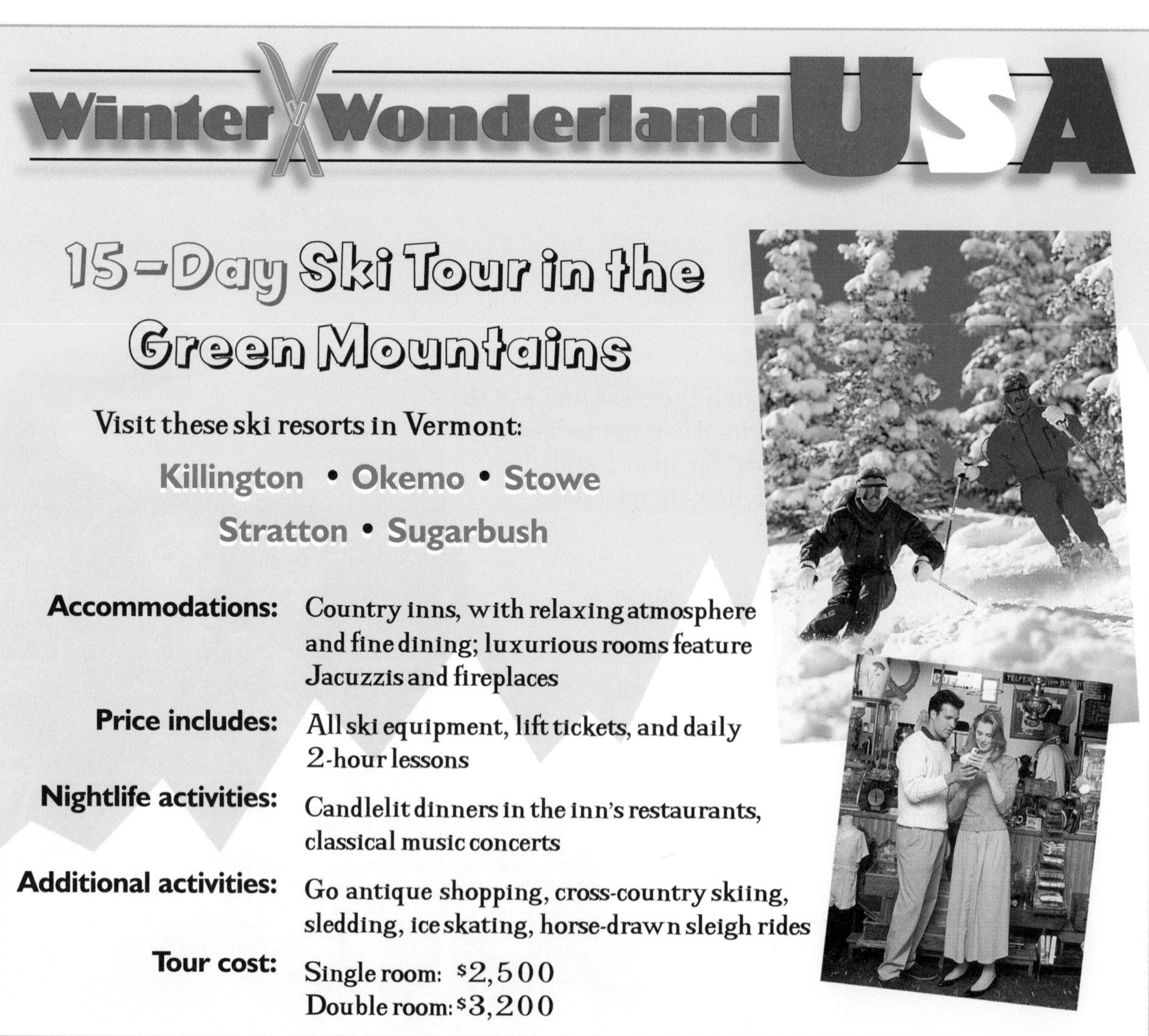

Winter Wonderland USA
15-Day Ski Tour in the Green Mountains
Visit these ski resorts in Vermont:
Killington • Okemo • Stowe
Stratton • Sugarbush
Accommodations: Country inns, with relaxing atmosphere and fine dining; luxurious rooms feature Jacuzzis and fireplaces
Price includes: All ski equipment, lift tickets, and daily 2-hour lessons
Nightlife activities: Candlelit dinners in the inn's restaurants, classical music concerts
Additional activities: Go antique shopping, cross-country skiing, sledding, ice skating, horse-drawn sleigh rides
Tour cost: Single room: $2,500
Double room: $3,200

C ***Pair work*** Decide which trip you are going to take. Then explain your choice to the class.

interchange 6 THAT'S NO EXCUSE!

A ***Pair work*** Look at these situations and act out conversations. Apologize and then give an excuse, admit a mistake, make an offer, or make a promise.

1

Student A: You're the customer.
Student B: You're the hairstylist.

A: My hair! You ruined my hair!
B: I'm so sorry. I . . . .

2

Student A: You own the puppy.
Student B: You own the backpack.

3

Student A: You're driving the red car.
Student B: You're driving the blue car.

4

Student A: You're the customer.
Student B: You're the cashier.

B ***Group work*** Have you ever experienced situations like these? What happened? What did you do? Share your stories.

interchange 5 FUN VACATIONS

Student B

A ***Pair work*** You and your partner are going to take a trip. You have a brochure for a surfing trip, and your partner has a brochure for a ski trip. First, use the information in this brochure to answer your partner's questions about the surfing trip.

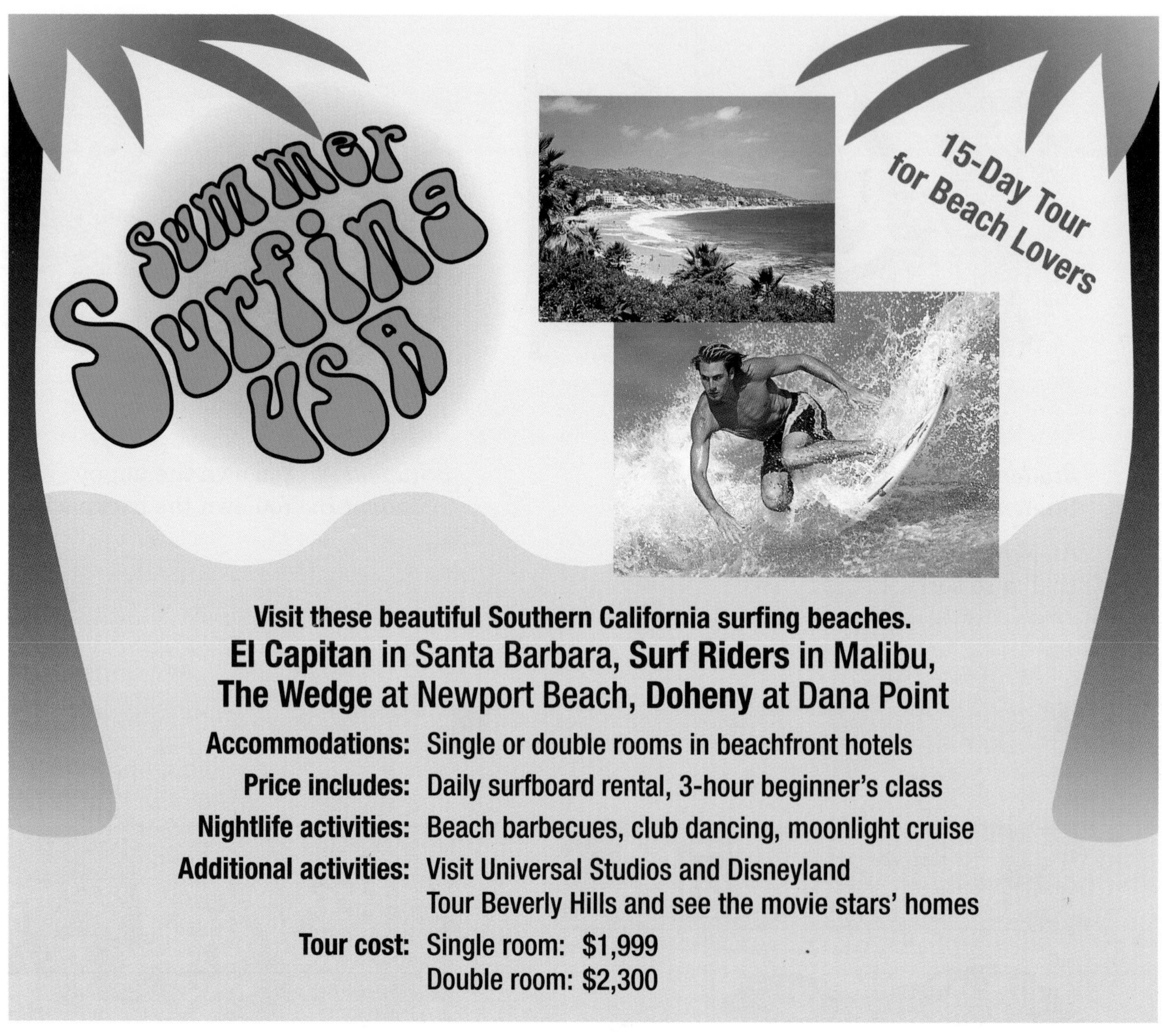

Summer Surfing USA
15-Day Tour for Beach Lovers
Visit these beautiful Southern California surfing beaches.
El Capitan in Santa Barbara, Surf Riders in Malibu,
The Wedge at Newport Beach, Doheny at Dana Point
Accommodations: Single or double rooms in beachfront hotels
Price includes: Daily surfboard rental, 3-hour beginner's class
Nightlife activities: Beach barbecues, club dancing, moonlight cruise
Additional activities: Visit Universal Studios and Disneyland
Tour Beverly Hills and see the movie stars' homes
Tour cost: Single room: $1,999
Double room: $2,300

B ***Pair work*** Now ask questions like these about the ski trip:

How much does the trip cost?
What does the price of the trip include?
What are the accommodations like?
Are skiing lessons available?
Is there going to be anything else to do? Tell me about the nightlife.
What else can you tell me about the trip?

C ***Pair work*** Decide which trip you are going to take. Then explain your choice to the class.

interchange 7 GOOD ADVICE

Student A

A ***Pair work*** Ask your partner for advice about these situations.

I'm going away on vacation and my house will be empty. How can I make my house safe from burglars?

I'm buying a used car. How can I make sure that it's in good condition?

I have an important job interview. How can I make a good impression?

- look presentable
- sound confident
- give an assured hand-shake

A: I'm going away on vacation and my house will be empty.
How can I make my house safe from burglars?
B: Well, don't forget to lock all the windows. Oh, and make sure to . . . .

B ***Pair work*** Now your partner needs advice about these situations. Give at least four suggestions for each one.

useful expressions	
Don't forget to	Try not to . . . .
Remember to	Make sure to . . . .
Try to	Be sure not to . . . .

BOOKS

Your partner is going to rent an apartment with a roommate.

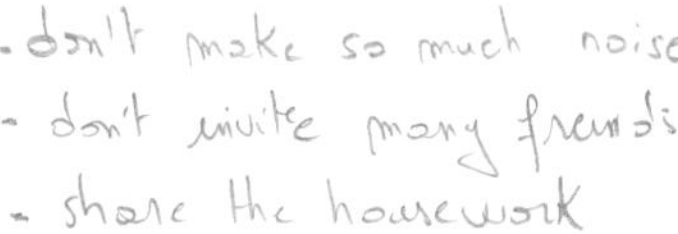
- don't make so much noise
- don't invite many friends
- share the housework

Your partner is meeting his girlfriend's or her boyfriend's parents for the first time.

be charming

Your partner is mailing a valuable glass vase to a friend.

interchange 7 GOOD ADVICE

Student B

A ***Pair work*** Your partner needs advice about these situations. Give at least four suggestions for each one.

useful expressions	
Don't forget to	Try not to . . . .
Remember to	Make sure to . . . .
Try to	Be sure not to . . . .

Your partner is going away on vacation and his or her house will be empty.

Your partner is buying a used car.

Your partner has an important job interview.

A: I'm going away on vacation and my house will be empty. How can I make my house safe from burglars?
B: Well, don't forget to lock all the windows. Oh, and make sure to . . . .

B ***Pair work*** Now ask your partner for advice about these situations.

I'm going to rent an apartment with a roommate. What can we do to get along well?

I'm meeting my girlfriend's/boyfriend's parents for the first time. How can I make a good impression?

I'm mailing a valuable glass vase to my friend. How can I make sure it arrives safely?

interchange 8 ONCE IN A BLUE MOON

A ***Class activity*** How do your classmates celebrate special days and times? Go around the class and ask the questions below. If someone answers "Yes," write down his or her name. Ask for more information and take notes.

A: Does your family have big get-togethers?
B: Yes, we do.
A: What do you do when you get together?
B: Well, we have a big meal. After we eat, we watch old home movies.

	Name	Notes
1. Does your family have big get-togethers?		
2. Do you ever buy flowers for someone special?		
3. Do you often take friends out to dinner?		
4. Do you wear your national dress at least once a year?		
5. Has someone given you money recently as a gift?		
6. Have you given money to someone recently as a gift?		
7. Do you like to celebrate your birthday with a party?		
8. Do you ever send birthday cards?		
9. Do you ever give friends birthday presents?		
10. Do you think long engagements are a good idea?		
11. Do you drink champagne at special events?		
12. Is New Year's your favorite time of the year?		
13. Do you ever celebrate a holiday with fireworks?		

B ***Pair work*** Compare your information with a partner.

Unit Summaries

Units Summaries contain lists of key vocabulary and functional expressions, as well as grammar extensions for each unit. For Grammar Focus models, please refer to the appropriate unit page.

1 A TIME TO REMEMBER

KEY VOCABULARY

Nouns
attic
(soccer) ball
beach
bicycle
(summer) camp
cat
chess
child
childhood
college
comic
dog
family
friend
hide-and-seek
hobby
immigrant
job
kid
lesson
memory
parents
park
pet
picture
place
possession
rabbit
scrapbook
shell
town
tree house
uncle
vacation
violin

Pronouns
that
this
yourself

Adjectives
big
favorite
fine
first
fun
good (at . . .)
great
near
OK
old
scary
second
small

Verbs
Modals
can
could
would

Other
be
begin
collect
follow
get up
give
go
grow up
have (a . . . time)
learn
move
paint
play
Rollerblade
spend (time)
stay
study
think
throw out
walk

Adverbs
ago
always
early
every (day)
here
just
most
neither
not anymore
now
only
originally
pretty
really
still
there
too
very

Prepositions
about (yourself)
after (school)
along (the beach)
at (his house)
from (South America)
in (high school)
in front of
to (college)

Conjunctions
and
but

Interjections
by the way
hey
in fact
oh
say
wow

EXPRESSIONS

Greeting someone
Hi./Hello.

Introducing yourself
My name is . . . /I'm . . .
Nice to meet you.
Good to meet you, too.

Exchanging personal information
Could you tell me (a little) about yourself?
Sure. What do you want to know?
Are you from . . . ?
Yes, I am./No, I'm not.
Where were you born?
I was born in . . . .
Did you grow up there?
Did you go to school in . . . ?
Yes, I did./No, I didn't.

Talking about past activities
Where did you learn to . . . ?
Here.
How old were you when you began to . . . ?
I was . . . years old.
What/Where did you use to . . . ?
When I was a kid, I used to . . . .
I used to . . . , too, when I was a kid.

Talking about past abilities
How well did you . . . ?
I was pretty good.

Apologizing
I'm (really) sorry.

Asking for and agreeing to a favor
Can you . . . ?
Sure.

Giving opinions
I bet . . . .

GRAMMAR EXTENSION *Adverbial clauses with* when

These four sentences mean the same; here, *when* means "at that time":

a) **When** I was in high school, we moved here.
b) We moved here **when** I was in high school.
c) **When** we moved here, I was in high school.
d) I was in high school **when** we moved here.

When an adverbial clause comes before an independent clause (as in sentences a and c), a comma is used.

2 CAUGHT IN THE RUSH

KEY VOCABULARY

Nouns
City places
airport
bank
cash machine
dance club
department store
(business) district
newsstand
restaurant
(duty-free) shop

Transportation
bicycle
(lane/stand)
bus
(lane/station/stop)
car
subway
(entrance/station)
taxi
(driver/lane/stand)
train

Other
certificate
coffee
counter
crime
cup
facility
fare
fire
government
hall
hamburger
highway
(half) hour
idea
letter
location
ma'am
(news)paper
noise
parking
(garage/light/space)
pedestrian
police (officer)
(air) pollution
question
restroom
route
rush hour
stop (light/sign)
street (light/sign)
system
telephone
traffic
(light/sign/jam)

Pronoun
one

Adjectives
average
cheap
close (to)
full
polite
public
special
sure
terrible
terrific
wrong

Verbs
Modal
be able to
should

Other
arrive
be allowed (to)
buy
check
come
cost
drive
feel like
find
get
improve
leave (for)
look
move
need
open
park
provide
see
take (time)
talk about
write

Adverbs
downtown
in general
much
never
quickly
right
sometimes
upstairs

Prepositions
across from
around (here)
at (rush hour)
behind
down (the hall)
except
on (the corner of)
next to

Conjunctions
however
so

Interjection
oh, no

EXPRESSIONS

Expressing a concern
There are too many . . . ./There is too much . . . .
There aren't enough . . . ./There isn't enough . . . .
We need more . . . .
There should be fewer . . . ./There should be less . . . .

Getting someone's attention
Excuse me.

Asking for and giving information
Can you tell me where . . . ?
Let me think.
Could you tell me how often . . . ?
Every . . . .
Do you know what time/when . . . ?
Sorry. I don't know.
Just one more thing.
Yes?

Asking a rhetorical question
Why is there never a . . . when you need one?
Good question.

Thanking someone
Thanks (a lot).

Making a suggestion
Let's (go and) . . . .

Expressing probability
It should . . . .

GRAMMAR EXTENSION Word order with Wh-words

Direct question

Where	is	the bank?
Wh-word	verb	subject

Indirect question

Do you know	where	the bank	is?
	Wh-word	subject	verb

Statement

I don't know	where	the bank	is.
	Wh-word	subject	verb

3 TIME FOR A CHANGE!

KEY VOCABULARY

Nouns
Houses / Apartments
bathroom
bedroom
closet
kitchen
living room
window

Other
appearance
(rock) band
class
clothes
guitar
homework
interest
leisure
life
(a) lot (of)
money
musician
neighborhood
personality
skill

Pronouns
something
somewhere

Adjectives
Describing houses and apartments
bright
comfortable
convenient
cramped
dangerous
dark
dingy
expensive
huge
inconvenient
large
modern
new
noisy
private
quiet
reasonable
safe
shabby
spacious

Other
boring
different
difficult
easy
free
healthy
in (good) shape
last
own
part-time
single

Verbs
Modal
have to

Other
add
become
change
do (chores)
enjoy
go back
go out
like
live
make (friends)
pay
read
rent
retire
show
take (classes)
work

Adverbs
a little
actually
all (day)
else
not at all
then
well

Prepositions
around (the house)
in (the evening)

Conjunction
though

Interjections
hmm
uh

EXPRESSIONS

Asking for and giving an opinion
What do you think?
The . . . isn't . . . enough.
The . . . is too . . . .
There aren't enough . . . ./There isn't enough . . . .
It's not as . . . as . . . .
It doesn't have as many . . . as . . . ./ It has just as many . . . as . . . .

Exchanging personal information
Where are you working now?
I'm still at the . . . .
How old are you?
(I'm) . . . .

Expressing regret about a present situation
I wish (that) I could . . . .
I wish I didn't . . . .
I wish life were easier.

Expressing sympathy and empathy
That's too bad.
I know what you mean.

Agreeing
I don't . . . either.

Expressing interest
Really?

GRAMMAR EXTENSION Evaluations

Evaluations often include an infinitive (*to* + base verb).

adjective + enough + *infinitive*
The kitchen isn't **large enough to eat in.**

too + *adjective* + *infinitive*
The kitchen is **too small to eat in.**

4 I'VE NEVER HEARD OF THAT!

KEY VOCABULARY

Nouns
Food and beverages
bagel
banana
beef
brains
bread
cake
chicken
coconut milk
curry
(scrambled) egg
eggplant
fish
frog's legs
garlic
guacamole (dip)
honey
meat
(coconut) milk
oil
onion
pasta
peanut butter
pizza
popcorn
potato
sandwich
shrimp
snails
soup
vegetable
water

Meals
breakfast
dinner
lunch

Other
appetizer
barbecue
bowl
charcoal
check
diet
dish
ingredient
kebob
lighter fluid
marinade
menu
picnic
(food) poisoning
recipe
skewer
slice
snack
sir

Adjectives
awful
barbecued
delicious
fried
interesting
strange
toasted

Verbs
Cooking methods
bake
barbecue
boil
fry
roast
steam

Other
cut into/up
decide (on)
eat
hear of
light
make (= prepare)
marinate
pour (over)
prefer
put in/on
skip
spread
take off
try
turn over

Adverbs
ever
from time to time
lately
recently
usually
yesterday
yet

Prepositions
for (20 minutes)
in (the morning)

EXPRESSIONS

Talking about food and beverages
Have you ever eaten . . . ?
Yes, I have./No, I haven't.
It's/They're . . . !
This/It sounds . . . ./They sound . . . .
Yum!
Ugh!/Yuck!

Ordering in a restaurant
Have you decided yet?
Yes. I'll have . . . .
And you?
I think I'll have the . . . .

Making and declining an offer
Like to . . . ?
No, thanks.

Describing a procedure
First, ...
Then . . . .
Next, ...
After that, ...
Finally, ...

Stating a preference
I usually like to . . . .
I prefer to . . . .

GRAMMAR EXTENSION *Two meanings of* recently

In the present perfect, *recently* means "during the period of days or weeks" or "lately."

I've eaten out a lot **recently** – three times this week.

In the past tense, *recently* means "not long ago."

I **recently** ate Korean food for the first time – last week, in fact.

5 GOING PLACES

KEY VOCABULARY

Nouns
Activities
camping
fishing
hiking
mountain climbing
rafting
reading
swimming

Other
backpack
(hiking) boots
camper
cash
condominium
country
cousin
credit card
culture
expedition
father
first-aid kit
identification
lots (of)
luggage
medication
mom
overnight bag
national park
passport
plan
plenty (of)
pocket
(hotel) reservation
shorts
suitcase
temple
thing
(plane) ticket
traveler's check
trip
vaccination
visa
wallet
weather
week
windbreaker
world

Pronoun
anyone

Adjectives
alone
back
excited
exciting
foreign
pleasant
round-trip
several
warm

Verbs
Modals
had better
must
ought to
should

Other
backpack
carry
catch up on
check on
have (time off)
lie
pack
start
take (a vacation/a walk)
think (about/of)
travel
visit

Adverbs
abroad
already
around
away
lots of
maybe
nearby
probably
so

Prepositions
around (Europe)
by (yourself)
for (a few days)

EXPRESSIONS

Talking about definite plans
Have you made any plans?
I'm going to . . . .

Talking about possible plans
What are you going to do?
I guess/I think I'll . . . .
I'll probably . . . .
Maybe I'll . . . .

Asking about length of time
For how long?
How long are you going to . . . ?
How long should we . . . ?

Expressing necessity
You (don't) have to/You must/You need to . . . .

Making a suggestion
You'd better . . . .
You ought to/should/shouldn't . . . .

Making and accepting an offer
Why don't you . . . ?
Do you mean it? I'd love to!

GRAMMAR EXTENSION Future sentences

With present continuous

The present continuous is often used with a future meaning when we are talking about things that have already been decided on and planned.

Where **are** you **going** for your vacation?
We're **staying** home. My grandparents **are coming** for a visit.

With simple present

The simple present is often used with a future meaning when we are talking about timetables, schedules, and so on.

When **do** you **leave**?
Our plane **takes off** at midnight, and we **arrive** in Paris at 7:00 A.M.

6 SURE. NO PROBLEM!

KEY VOCABULARY

Nouns
block
cigarette
coat
(a) couple (of)
dollar
driveway
dry cleaning
faucet
floor
garbage
groceries
lasagna
magazine
mess
music
neighbor
oven
phone
problem
program
radio
(non-smoking) section
shoe
sound
stereo
towel
toy
trash
TV
wall

Pronoun
anything

Adjectives
broke
busy
loud
thin

Verbs
Two-part verbs
clean off/up
hang up
keep down
move into
pay back
pick up
put away/out
take off/out
throw out
turn down/off/on

Other
afford
block
drive
forget
help
lend
mind
plan (to)
realize
smoke

Adverbs
across
definitely
down
next door
(all) over
quietly
soon
through
tomorrow
totally

Prepositions
in (a minute)
on (the phone)

Conjunction
if

EXPRESSIONS

Making and agreeing/objecting to a request
Please . . . .
  Sure. No problem!
  Oh, but . . . .
Can/Could you . . . ?
  I'd be glad to.
Would you please . . . ?
  OK. I'll . . . .
Would you mind . . . ?
  Sorry. I'll . . . right away.

Apologizing
I'm sorry. I didn't realize./I forgot./I'll . . . right away.

Making a promise
I'll make sure to . . . .

Expressing annoyance
Goodness!

Expressing surprise
Are you kidding?

GRAMMAR EXTENSION Separable and inseparable two-part verbs

Some two-part verbs take a direct object and can be separated.

Put away your things.
Why don't you **put** your things **away**?
  I already **put** them **away**.

Other two-part verbs can also take direct objects but can't be separated.

Help me **look for** my new Suzanne Vega CD. I want to **listen to** it.
  Suzanne Vega? I never **heard of** her.

7 WHAT'S THIS FOR?

KEY VOCABULARY

Nouns
Machines / Appliances
battery
camcorder
CD-ROM
(laptop) computer
fax (machine)
hair dryer
microwave oven
modem
(cellular) phone
robot
satellite

Other
advice
astronomy
ATM card
attendance
behavior
(household) bill
budget
(send) button
(phone/telephone) call
chat (group/room)
cold
container
criminal
document
encyclopedia
factory
(DNA) fingerprinting
heat
in-line skate
information
instructions
Internet
jet ski
(phone) line
medical school
metal
mother
motorbike
movie
number
order
(electrical) outlet
paper (= composition)
(crime) pattern
people
person
photocopy
professor
psychotherapist
report
report card
(work) schedule
sport
task
UFO
worker
World Wide Web

Pronouns
mine
ours

Adjectives
closed
extreme
fragile
latest

Verbs
access
analyze
belong
communicate
connect
create
dial
drop
exchange
expose
get on
heat
identify
make sure
perform
place
plug
press
process
recharge
remember
research
run (a machine)
save
send
spill
store
teach
unplug
use

Adverbs
away
facedown
first of all
just about
often
on-line

Prepositions
at (a medical school)
in (a factory)
on (= about)

Interjection
uh-huh

EXPRESSIONS

Making a suggestion
Why don't you . . . ?
Maybe I will.

Describing a use or purpose
What's this for?
It's used for . . . ./It's used to . . . .
I can use it for . . . ./I can use it to . . . .
What are these for?
They're used for . . . ./They're used to . . . .
You can use them for . . . ./You can use them to . . . .

Giving and responding to advice
First of all, don't forget to . . . .
Got it!
Then . . . . And remember to . . . .
That's all?
Pretty much. Just make sure to . . . . And try not to . . . .
Good advice.

GRAMMAR EXTENSION Uncompleted infinitives

Advice
Remember to recharge the batteries.

Response with completed infinitive
I won't **forget to recharge** them.

Response with uncompleted infinitive (to avoid repetition)
I won't **forget to**.

8 LET'S CELEBRATE!

KEY VOCABULARY

Nouns
Holidays, festivals, and celebrations
anniversary
April Fool's Day
bachelor party
birthday
bridal shower
Carnival
engagement
Halloween
May Day
Mother's Day
New Year's Eve
party
(wedding) reception
Thanksgiving
Valentine's Day
wedding

Other
bride
candy
card
champagne
costume
couple
cranberry sauce
dancing
door
dress
fireworks
flower
gift
groom
kimono
man
mask
newlywed
night
occasion
part
period
photo
present
revolution
samba
trick
turkey
woman
word

Seasons
fall
spring
summer
winter

Pronouns
each other
everyone
ones

Adjectives
beautiful
engaged
female
long
male
Western
white
young

Verbs
ask for
attend
celebrate
change (into)
date
dress up
get
(engaged/married/
together)
happen
have (a party)
hold
honor
invite
knock
last
love
party
receive
return
say
serve
wear

Adverb
on . . . own

Prepositions
by (saying)
during (the reception)
on (October 31st)
with (cranberry sauce)

Interjection
Trick or treat!

EXPRESSIONS

Describing holidays, festivals, and celebrations
. . . is a day/a night when . . . .
. . . is the day when . . . .
. . . is the season when . . . .
A . . . is a time when . . . .
. . . is the month when . . . .
Before . . . , ...
After . . . , ...
When . . . , ...

Asking about customs
How old are people when they . . . ?
Is there . . . ?
Where is the . . . usually held?
What happens during the . . . ?
What do . . . wear?
What type of food is served?

GRAMMAR EXTENSION Adverbial clauses of time

In sentences with clauses beginning with *before* and *after*, there is always one action that comes before another.

Before a man gets married, his friends give him a party. = First, his friends give him a party; then he gets married.

After a woman gets married, she often changes her name. = First, she gets married; then she changes her name.

With clauses beginning with *when*, however, either one action comes before another – and *when* means "after" – or both actions happen at the same time.

When a woman gets married, she often changes her name. = First, she gets married; then she changes her name.

When a woman gets married, she usually wears a white dress. = During the time she's getting married, she wears a white dress. (both happen at the same time)

Appendix

COUNTRIES AND NATIONALITIES

This is a partial list of countries, many of which are presented in this book.

Country	Nationality
Argentina	Argentine
Australia	Australian
Austria	Austrian
Brazil	Brazilian
Bolivia	Bolivian
Canada	Canadian
Chile	Chilean
China	Chinese
Colombia	Colombian
Costa Rica	Costa Rican
Ecuador	Ecuadorian
Egypt	Egyptian
England	English
France	French
Germany	German
Greece	Greek
Hungary	Hungarian
India	Indian
Indonesia	Indonesian
Ireland	Irish
Italy	Italian
Japan	Japanese
Korea	Korean
Lebanon	Lebanese
Malaysia	Malaysian
Mexico	Mexican
Morocco	Moroccan
New Zealand	New Zealander
the Philippines	Filipino
Poland	Polish
Russia	Russian
Singapore	Singaporean
Spain	Spanish
Switzerland	Swiss
Thailand	Thai
Turkey	Turkish
Peru	Peruvian
the United Kingdom	British
the United States	American
Uruguay	Uruguayan

NUMBERS

0 zero	1 one	2 two	3 three	4 four	5 five	6 six	7 seven	8 eight
9 nine	10 ten	11 eleven	12 twelve	13 thirteen	14 fourteen	15 fifteen	16 sixteen	17 seventeen
18 eighteen	19 nineteen	20 twenty	21 twenty-one	22 twenty-two	30 thirty	40 forty	50 fifty	60 sixty
70 seventy	80 eighty	90 ninety	100 one hundred (a hundred)			1,000 one thousand (a thousand)		

COMPARATIVE AND SUPERLATIVE ADJECTIVES

1. Adjective with *-er* and *-est*

big	dirty	high	old	tall
busy	dry	hot	pretty	ugly
cheap	easy	large	quiet	warm
clean	fast	light	safe	wet
close	friendly	long	scary	young
cold	funny	mild	short	
cool	great	new	slow	
deep	heavy	nice	small	

2. Adjectives with *more* and *most*

attractive	exciting	outgoing
beautiful	expensive	popular
boring	famous	relaxing
crowded	important	stressful
dangerous	interesting	difficult
delicious		

3. Irregular adjectives

good → better → best
bad → worse → the worst

PRONUNCIATION OF REGULAR PAST FORMS

with /d/	*with* /t/	with /ɪd/
studied	worked	invited
stayed	watched	visited

IRREGULAR VERBS

Present	*Past*	*Participle*	*Present*	*Past*	*Participle*
(be) am/is, are	was, were	been	make	made	made
become	became	become	meet	met	met
break	broke	broken	pay	paid	paid
bring	brought	brought	put	put	put
build	built	built	quit	quit	quit
buy	bought	bought	read	read	read
come	came	come	ride	rode	ridden
cost	cost	cost	ring	rang	rung
cut	cut	cut	run	ran	run
do	did	done	say	said	said
drink	drank	drunk	see	saw	seen
drive	drove	driven	sell	sold	sold
eat	ate	eaten	send	sent	sent
fall	fell	fallen	set	set	set
feel	felt	felt	sit	sat	sat
fight	fought	fought	sleep	slept	slept
find	found	found	speak	spoke	spoken
fly	flew	flown	spend	spent	spent
forget	forgot	forgotten	stand	stood	stood
get	got	gotten	steal	stole	stolen
give	gave	given	swim	swam	swum
go	went	gone	take	took	taken
grow	grew	grown	teach	taught	taught
have	had	had	tell	told	told
hear	heard	heard	think	thought	thought
hold	held	held	wear	wore	worn
keep	kept	kept	win	won	won
lend	lent	lent	write	wrote	written
lose	lost	lost			

Acknowledgments

ILLUSTRATIONS

Randy Jones 2, 3, 8, 14, 29, 34 38, 43, 45, IC-2, IC-3, IC-7, IC-9 *(top)*, IC-10 *(top)*

Mark Kaufman 14, 15, 22, 23, 31 *(top)* 35, 36 99, *(bottom)*, 44, 49

Kevin Spaulding 5, 28, 34 *(bottom)*, 40, 52

Sam Viviano 6, 11, 17, 18, 20, 27, 31 *(bottom)*, 36 *(top)*, 37, 47, 52 *(top)*, 53, IC-4, IC-5, IC-9 *(bottom)*, IC-10 *(bottom)*

PHOTOGRAPHIC CREDITS

The authors and publishers are grateful for permission to reproduce the following photographs. Every endeavor has been made to contact copyright owners, and apologies are expressed for omissions.

2 © Remi Benali/Gamma Liaison

5 *(left)* © Mug Shots/The Stock Market; *(right)* © Ariel Skelley/The Stock Market

6 © Tony Freeman/PhotoEdit

7 *(left)* © Globe Photos; *(right)* © Barry King/Gamma Liaison

8 *(left)* © Patti McConville/The Image Bank; *(right)* © Grant V. Faint/The Image Bank

9 © Dick Luria/FPG International

12 © Michael Yamashita/Gamma Liaison

13 *(left to right)* Jeff Greenberg/Omni Photo Communications; courtesy of Netherlands Board of Tourism; © Hugo de Vries, courtesy of State of Hawaii Department of Transportation

19 *(left)* PEOPLE Weekly © 1996 Ed Lallo; *(right)* © Mel Neale

20 (feijoada) © Paulo Fridman/International Stock; (mee krob and won ton soup) From Sunset Oriental Cookbook, © 1970, Sunset Books Inc., Menlo Park, CA; (ceviche) © Peter Johansky/Envision

21 © Bill Bachmann/PhotoEdit

24 *(left to right)* © Joel Glenn/The Image Bank; © Ed Bock/The Stock Market; © David Jeffrey/The Image Bank; © Roy Morsch/The Stock Market

25 © Steven Needham/Envision

26 *(both)* © SuperStock

27 © Le Goy/Gamma Liaison

30© David Ball/Tony Stone Images

32 © Telegraph Colour Library/FPG International

33 *(top)* © Alan Becker/The Image Bank; *(bottom)* © German Youth Hostel Assoc./HI-AYH

39 *(left)* © Beth Whitman, courtesy of The Fresh Air Fund; *(right)* © Jeffrey Sylvester/FPG International

41 *(top to bottom)* © G.S.O. Images/The Image Bank; © David Ash/Tony Stone Images; © Garry Gay/The Image Bank

42 *(left to right)* © Richard Nowitz/FPG International; © Zigy Kaluzny/Tony Stone Images; © Flip Chalfant/The Image Bank

43 (microwave and hair dryer) ourtesy of Sears, Roebuck and Co.; (laptop computer) courtesy of IBM Corporation

44 *(top row, left to right)* courtesy of Sears, Roebuck and Co.; courtesy of Yamaha Motor Corporation, U.S.A.; courtesy of Sears, Roebuck and Co.; *(bottom row, left to right)* courtesy of Rollerblade, Inc.; courtesy of The Long Island Savings Bank; courtesy of Kawasaki Motors Corp., U.S.A.

48 *(top to bottom)* © Ary Diesendruck/Tony Stone Images; © Martha Cooper/Viesti Associates; © Robert Frerck/Tony Stone Images; © Ron Behrmann/International Stock

49 © Satoru Ohmori/Gamma Liaison

50 *(clockwise from top right)* © Paul Chesley/Tony Stone Images; © Josef Beck/FPG International; © Spencer Grant/Gamma Liaison

51 *(left to right)* © Robert Frerck/Odyssey Productions/Chicago; courtesy of Korean Cultural Service; © AP/Wide World Photos

IC-6 *(top)* © Ken Gallard/International Stock; *(bottom)* © John Michael/International Stock

IC-8 *(top)* © Lorentz Gullachsen/Tony Stone Images; *(bottom)* © Robert Brown/International Stock

IC-11 *(left to right)* © Jon Riley/Tony Stone Images; © Rob Lewine/ The Stock Market; © John Pinderhughes/The Stock Market